British Railway Picto

Black Country

Paul Collins

Ian Allan
PUBLISHING

CONTENTS

INTRODUCTION

Anyone who writes anything about the Black Country feels almost compelled to define it — and that is not easy. 'The Black Country' is a term that has been applied to that part of what historically was South Staffordshire and East Worcestershire, to the west of Birmingham and to the south of Wolverhampton. In many ways it is the expression on the surface of the area's 10yd-thick seam of coal, upon which much of its wealth was founded. But things are not that simple. There is also a sense in which the Black Country can be defined by what it does not include, born of people's attitudes towards the name and all that it conveys. For example, Stourbridge long considered itself too grand to be part of the Black Country, but it most assuredly was and is, whereas historically Wolverhampton was not part of it, but has at times enthusiastically appended a 'Welcome to the Black Country' tag to many of its signs.

This book is a collection of photographs of various ages showing the railways of the Black Country and the impact they once had on work and life there. It is not intended as a definitive history of the subject. Others, including this author, have been there already. Compiling it has served as a reminder of the debt owed to those who photographed these everyday scenes up to 50 or more years ago. Howsoever self-conscious they might have felt at the time, we can have nothing but gratitude to Mike Mensing, Ron Moss, Neil Pitts and the others whose work is reproduced here, for the many hours they must have spent standing on embankments, bridges, and other 'perches' in all weathers, waiting for that perfect moment when train, light and framing all came together.

Thanks are offered to the following individuals and organisations, without whose kind assistance and generosity this book would not have been possible: Lawrie Bowles; June Collins; Ray Cresswell and Brierley Office Products; Paul Cripps; Tom Ferris; Nick Grant; Katherine Hamer; Mellanie Hartland; Stan Hill; Ian Allan Publishing Ltd; Michael Mensing; Ron Moss; the late Neil Pitts; Brian Standish and Peter Waller.

Paul Collins
Wollaston, Stourbridge
August 2003

Title page: **The GWR withdrew its public passenger service between Old Hill and Halesowen on 5 December 1927, but the station was sustained by workmen's trains to 'The Austin' works at Longbridge and by parcels and goods traffic. This track-level view was recorded in the mid-1950s.**
K. D. Shakespeare

First published 2003

ISBN 0 7110 2969 5

Published by Ian Allan Publishing

an imprint of Ian Allan Publishing Ltd, Hersham, Surrey KT12 4RG.
Printed by Ian Allan Printing Ltd, Hersham, Surrey KT12 4RG.

Code: 0310/B

Above: **'56xx' 0-6-2T No 6674 trundles between Lye and Cradley Heath with a short down freight on 14 June 1958. The sidings served fireclay mines at Netherend, whilst one of the area's many firebrick works can be seen on the skyline to the right.** *Michael Mensing*

1. BEGINNINGS

Lacking any navigable rivers, the Black Country had to wait until the advent of the canals before its vast mineral wealth of coal, fireclay, and limestone could be exploited, and this began with the opening of the Staffordshire & Worcestershire Canal on 28 May 1772. The only completed work of James Brindley, this opened up the Black Country to outside markets and sowed the seed for vast fortunes to be made. This canal — and the many others that followed it — was fed by the Black Country's roads, which, much as today, proved inadequate in the face of ever-increasing traffic. It was perhaps inevitable, therefore, that other means of feeding canals should be tried. One such was a railway. Railways were not new to the area. One of the earliest recorded was built in 1665 to link mines in Pensnett to the River Stour near Stourbridge, but it had wooden rails and used horse power. The lines proposed in the first quarter of the 19th century were different — they would use steam locomotives.

Between 1819 and 1831 the Black Country benefited from the partnership between the inventive genius of engineer John Urpeth Rastrick and the entrepreneurial skills of ironmaster James Foster. Rastrick was a friend of locomotive pioneer Richard Trevithick, while Foster was heir to the ironworks and fortune of John Bradley & Co in Stourbridge. Foster owned collieries at Shutt End, near Kingswinford, and planned blast furnaces there; these would serve (and be served by) the main works in Stourbridge. The only problem was that the roads linking Shutt End and Stourbridge were amongst the busiest in the district, being the main route to Wolverhampton and the axis along which many of the area's glassworks were arrayed.

Rastrick's solution was simple — ignore the roads! Instead he planned a railway linking Shutt End with Ashwood on the Staffordshire & Worcestershire Canal, from where minerals could be transferred to and from canal boats. The line had an inclined plane at each end, but its central section, with a ruling gradient of 1 in 330 was considered sufficiently 'level' to permit the use of a steam locomotive. The Shutt End Railway was duly built between late 1826 and 1829, the line opening with much ceremony on

2 June 1829. Star of the day was Rastrick's locomotive — *The Agenoria* — which performed many runs along the line, culminating in pulling a train of 131½ tons — 11 times its own weight — which included no fewer than 920 persons, who somehow hung on as it 'rocketed' along at 3½ miles per hour! Research has since revealed that on 2 June 1829 *The Agenoria* was one of only 26 steam locomotives known to have been working in Britain at the time and the only one in the Midlands or the South of England. *The Agenoria* has survived and is the oldest intact locomotive in the National Collection at York.

The Shutt End line was just one of a number that Rastrick had planned for the Black Country, but none of the others was built, and the area had to wait almost 10 years before any more railways would

serve it. The Shutt End Railway became part of the Earl of Dudley's Pensnett Railway system. Begun in 1846 to connect New Level Furnaces in Brierley Hill with collieries at Old Park, this became one of the largest private mineral railways in the UK. The system, centred on the Earl of Dudley's Round Oak Iron & Steel Works, comprised almost 40 miles of track and was serviced by locomotive and wagon shops at The Wallows, which adjoined Round Oak.

In the late 1940s the Pensnett Railway began to contract as the mines it served became worked out. The original Shutt End line closed on 31 October 1953, but railway activity survived the closure of Round Oak Steelworks on 23 December 1982, as portions of the former Pensnett Railway survive as the base of Round Oak Rail Ltd, a distribution company.

Above: **Having played the leading role in the opening of the Shutt End Railway on 2 June 1829, *The Agenoria* enjoyed a working life of some 35 years. She spent as much time running backwards as forwards, as the line was single throughout! Sometime in April 1864 she came off the track, and, because the Pensnett Railway (of which the Shutt End had now become part) had newer locomotives, there she stayed until 'discovered' *c*1879. *The Agenoria* was restored at Pensnett Railway's Wallows workshops and is seen at Round Oak Iron & Steel Works on 8 September 1882 following this work.** *Stourbridge Library*

Above: **Although it is known that when** *The Agenoria* **was discovered she had her tender attached, this detail from the previous photograph also suggests that some of her wagons survived to this date. This is a close-up of one of these wagons. The similarity between the wheels and riveting on the wagon and those on** *The Agenoria*'s **tender is remarkable.** *Stourbridge Library*

Right: **After some uncertainty over her future,** *The Agenoria* **was donated in the early 1880s to the Patent Office Museum but found herself one of the first railway exhibits at The Science Museum in South Kensington, London, where she was formally received, with her tender, on 30 December 1884. The tender was cut up, as it took up too much room, but the locomotive eventually became a prized exhibit at the National Railway Museum in York, by way of all the major exhibitions of the first half of the 20th century. She is seen at York in the 1950s, probably** *enroute* **to or from the Festival of Britain in 1951.** *Author's collection*

Left: **Round Oak Iron & Steel Works was founded in 1857 on land situated between the Level Furnaces and the Oxford, Worcester & Wolverhampton Railway (OWW) at Round Oak, Brierley Hill. It became the hub of the Earl of Dudley's vast coal and iron empire, whose disparate elements were united by railways, the first of which were laid down in 1844. This is Round Oak in 1865, in a photograph taken for an illustrated book on Dudley. By this date three Manning Wardle 0-4-0 locomotives were employed to work the line, and it can reasonably be assumed that it is one of these that can be seen here.** *Author's collection*

Above left: **For many years wagons used on the Pensnett Railway carried the initials 'PR' or 'ED' (for Earl of Dudley) on their sides, but by 1958, when this photograph was taken, they carried just 'RO' (for Round Oak). Centre right, at top, one of the steelworks' Andrew Barclay locomotives reverses enthusiastically away from the camera, possibly having just been uncoupled from the line of wagons on the far right. The ramshackle nature of the scene belies the fact that Round Oak was still a thriving steelworks at this time, even though the cable-worked incline in the foreground looks as though is has not been used for years!** *Author's collection*

Below left: **The line to The Wallows Basin was known as the Pensnett branch and eventually gave its name to the whole Round Oak railway system. In reaching The Wallows the line crossed the alignment later adopted by the OWW, and, by virtue of being there first, crossed the main-line railway on the level. There was an air of resignation about this fact from the outset. As the OWW Bill passed through Parliament, I.K. Brunel was asked: 'Is it your intention to adopt your railway to the level of Lord Ward's Railway?', to which he replied: 'If Lord Ward will not alter his railway an inch, we must come to his.' The consequence of this is seen in May 1971, with the single-line Pensnett Railway curving across the main line from bottom left. The sight of a main-line train waiting for a small industrial locomotive with a few wagons behind to cross was one of the lost wonders of the Black Country.** *Neil Pitts/Author's collection*

Above right: **One of the first extensions proposed to the Earl of Dudley's Railway was a branch to connect with the head of his private canal — The Pensnett Canal — at The Wallows. This 1¼-mile level canal opened in 1840, and the railway connecting with it followed in 1845. The Wallows Basin is seen here in the 1920s. At the higher level, to the right, workmen help coal out of wagons on to an intermediate coaling stage, where a third workman discharges it into a waiting boat. Just how far these loaded boats were weighed down can be seen by comparison with the unladen one on the right.** *Author's collection*

Below right: **Until 1926 the majority of locomotive and wagon repair work on the Pensnett Railway had been undertaken at the works at Castle Mill. In that year all heavy repair work was transferred to enlarged sheds at The Wallows, seen here in May 1971, apparently in the midst of a clear-out. This building survives in 2003 as part of the industrial estate that has taken over the area.** *Neil Pitts/Author's collection*

Left: **The Pensnett Railway's Castle Mill Works was not just a repair shop; in 1902 it built its own locomotive,** *Edward VII,* **named in honour of the new King, who was crowned that year. The 0-4-0ST was rebuilt twice at Castle Mill, first in 1915 and again in 1924, and is seen here in its final form. Life was tough for locomotives on the Pensnett Railway, as the many dents and bent platework of** *Edward VII* **attest.** *Ian Allan Library (IAL)*

Centre left: **Only three locomotives were built at Castle Mill Works, the majority of those used on the Pensnett Railway being bought from the major locomotive builders. Andrew Barclay and Manning Wardle were favoured for 0-4-0s, but 0-6-0s, such as** *Lady Rosemary* **here, were obtained from the Hunslet Engine Co or, in this case, Peckett & Sons. One of two 0-6-0s bought in 1921,** *Lady Rosemary* **was used to replace cable haulage on Barrow Hill incline and performed this function until withdrawal in 1946, when she was scrapped.** *IAL*

Bottom left: **Second-hand locomotives were also used on the Pensnett Railway. No 15 was built by Peckett & Sons in 1889 and worked at Gwaun-cae-Gurwen Colliery until moving to Round Oak in February 1918. Partly rebuilt at Castle Mill Works in 1924, she worked on until 1934, when she was withdrawn and scrapped.** *IAL*

Right: **Only two Pensnett Railway locomotives were neither named nor numbered. This is therefore most likely to be a Peckett & Sons 0-4-0 which was scrapped in 1960. The short wheelbase of the locomotive would have suited it to the many curves on the Pensnett Railway.** *IAL*

Centre right: **The bulk of the Pensnett Railway's rolling stock consisted of open wooden-bodied mineral wagons, such as No 928, seen here in May 1971. These were obtained from the main-line railway companies, many being acquired shortly after World War2, just prior to the Nationalisation of the railways. These would have been maintained at The Wallows sheds, whose shops could accommodate up to 20 10-ton wagons at any one time.** *Neil Pitts/Author's collection*

Bottom right: **Some of the Pensnett Railway's rolling stock was specialised, such as these steel tippler wagons — Nos 335 and 348 — seen at The Wallows in May 1971. They were used to transport and tip hot ash from the furnaces, the remains of which can be seen caked to the wheels and brakes.** *Neil Pitts/Author's collection*

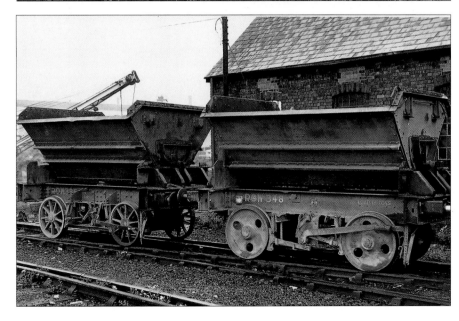

2. WOLVERHAMPTON

Wolverhampton gained its first railway and station because a line was built reasonably close by. Planned from 1831, the Grand Junction Railway (GJR) linked Birmingham with lines in the North West, including the world's first main-line railway, the Liverpool & Manchester. The GJR's engineers included John Urpeth Rastrick, who proposed a branch from the main line to Wolverhampton. In the event, this was not built, and the GJR's 'Wolverhampton' station was a mile northeast of the town, at Wednesfield Heath. It opened with the line, on 4 July 1837.

Wolverhampton was one of the fastest-growing towns in the UK, and within 10 years it became the scene of much railway construction and the 'field' upon which some fierce railway 'battles' were fought. 'Piggy-in-the-middle' was the Shrewsbury & Birmingham Railway Co (S&B), whose modest aim of linking its eponymous towns by rail put it at the centre of a struggle for supremacy between the companies allied to the Great Western Railway (GWR) and the London & North Western Railway (LNWR). At issue was the portion of the S&B between Wolverhampton and Birmingham, over which the GWR and LNWR camps fought. Despite this, in its 10 years'

existence (1844-54) the S&B played a major role in building both of Wolverhampton's main railway stations — High Level and Low Level — and one of its goods stations — Victoria Basin.

The disputed line between Wolverhampton and Birmingham was eventually built by the LNWR and would be forever known as the Stour Valley line — a name it gained from a branch to Stourbridge that was never constructed. The first main-line station in Wolverhampton itself was built jointly by the S&B and the LNWR. Originally known as Queen Street, after the thoroughfare at whose end it stood, it opened to passengers on 24 June 1852, one week ahead of the Stour Valley line.

Eventually the S&B sided with the GWR and became involved in building Wolverhampton's second main-line station. Built close to the LNWR station but on lower ground further from the town, this became known as 'Low Level' almost from its opening, the LNWR station becoming 'High Level'. Officially called the 'Wolverhampton Joint station' — from the joint involvement of the S&B, Oxford, Worcester & Wolverhampton (OWW) and Birmingham, Wolverhampton & Dudley (BWD) railways in its construction — Low Level opened on 1 July 1854. Its overall roof (removed in 1933/4) was the work of I. K. Brunel, and the station marked the most northerly point reached by the GWR's broad gauge.

The Midland Railway also gained a toehold in Wolverhampton, through its purchase on 1 July 1876 of the Wolverhampton & Walsall Railway (WWR), which it bought from the LNWR. The line had opened on 1 November 1872. Protracted wrangling over access to High Level station resulted in the Midland's planning its own Wolverhampton station on land beyond the Low Level station, but the town missed having its third ('Even Lower Level'?) station following agreement with the LNWR. The Midland used its 'station' site on the Wednesfield Road for a substantial goods station, which opened in November 1881.

Much of what the Victorians built was lost in the post-Beeching era of the 20th century. High Level station was rebuilt as part of the West Coast electrification scheme, with Low Level closing as a main-line station on the same day this came into public use — 6 March 1967. Closed to all passengers on 4 March 1972, Low Level survived first as a Parcels Concentration Depot — until 12 June 1981 — and then as a preserved listed building, until enthusiasm for its restoration waned in the mid-1980s. Ever since it has stood forlorn at the heart of administrative inertia and ever more crackpot schemes, none of which appears to recognise its significance and grandeur. Despite also being listed, Wednesfield Road Goods was demolished in the mid-1990s.

Above: **Wolverhampton's first railway station was one mile northeast of the town, at Wednesfield Heath, seen here in 1967, 94 years after the last passenger had used it. Superseded by the General (High Level) station from 24 June 1852, it closed to passengers on 1 September 1853 but was reopened to serve local trains between 1 August 1855 and 1 January 1873. The station building is the single-storey structure to the left of the lines, the larger building to the right being the station master's house.** *Author's collection*

Above left: **A second view of Wednesfield Heath station at platform level, taken in the 1950s just as a train hurtles through, possibly on an engineering diversion. Much of the surviving Grand Junction Railway infrastructure was swept away when this line was electrified. The new overhead wires came into use here in March 1966.** *Author's collection*

Above right: **It was long known that the Shrewsbury & Birmingham Railway opened to a temporary station on the Wednesfield Road on 12 November 1849, as work on the Wolverhampton General (later High Level) station had barely begun at that time. Use of the word 'temporary' has led many to speculate that this station must have been wooden, but in reality it was a substantial brick building that cost £380 to erect. Moreover, it remained, its significance overlooked, until the 1970s. Sadly, by the time that the true story emerged it was too late to photograph the temporary station, but this landscaped area shows where it stood.** *Author*

Centre right: **Despite the Shrewsbury & Birmingham Railway's involvement in building much of Wolverhampton's first generation of railway buildings, the company's legacy is the carriage-drive entrance to the original High Level station, now known as The Queen's Building. Originally accommodating the company's offices on the first floor, the building became the District Goods Manager's Office of the LNWR and (subsequently) the LMS, in which guise it is seen above in October 1938. Note the original gates behind the LMS excursion and savings notices.** *IAL*

Bottom right: **By 1966 the gates had been removed and the gateways they guarded bricked up. Used as a base for engineers working on the resignalling of the area in the early/mid-1960s, the offices were vacated early in 1971 and faced an uncertain future, which became even more so when the buildings on either side were demolished in July 1979.** *Lionel J. Lea*

Left: **The Queen's Building was given a Grade II listing on 3 February 1977 and eventually found a role as a café and enquiries office as part of Wolverhampton's new bus station. Restoration and conversion of the building began early in 1988, and this was the state of progress on 10 June that year. For a brief moment the original carriage-entrance archways were opened up, and the building could be appreciated in something akin to its original form.** *Author*

Centre left: **Both The Queen's Building and the General (High Level) station were the work of Wolverhampton architect Edward Banks. The similarity between the two can be appreciated by comparing this view from 1935 with those of The Queen's Building above and left. Opened on 24 June 1852, it was described in** *The Builder* **in 1861 as being 'made of the principal productions of the district, glass and iron, with no stint of either, or of anything else, substantial and satisfactory'. By 1935 the frontage carried a fascia board directing people to the GWR's Low Level station, down a rather treacherous tunnel, visible on the left.** *IAL*

Bottom left: **The opening of the Wolverhampton General station was delayed primarily by the difficulties surrounding construction of the Stour Valley line to Birmingham, which eventually opened on 1 July 1852. The furthest point along this line that can conceivably be regarded as being in the Black Country is Smethwick. Formed by a three-car Birmingham Railway & Carriage Works DMU set, the 18.05 Stoke-on-Trent–Birmingham service departs from Smethwick Rolfe Street station on 8 June 1961.** *Michael Mensing*

Right: **For much of its length between Oldbury and Coseley the Stour Valley line is carried level with or above the land it crosses. Forty years ago the view of factories and furnaces this afforded must have been fascinating, as passengers aboard the 10.30 Euston–Wolverhampton service on 30 July 1961 would have discovered. The train is seen south of Coseley & Deepfields station behind rebuilt 'Royal Scot' No 46111** *Royal Fusilier* **of 1943.**
Michael Mensing

Centre right: **Forming the most direct route between Birmingham and Wolverhampton, the Stour Valley line was electrified in the mid-1960s; work to erect the overhead gantries is well advanced as English Electric Type 4 1Co-Co1 diesel-electric locomotives Nos D375 and D322 haul a New Street-bound express through Coseley & Deepfields station on 5 June 1965. The overhead on this section of line was energised in October 1966, and electric trains first used it that December.**
Michael Mensing

Bottom right: **There were originally two stations between Coseley & Deepfields and Wolverhampton High Level — Ettingshall Road & Bilston and Monmore Green. The latter was closed from 1 January 1917, due to a shortage of labour caused by the Great War, and was not reopened. Ettingshall Road & Bilston remained open until 15 June 1964, closing in advance of the electrification and resignalling works then commencing; it was also probably the station from which Charles Dickens departed one wintry night in December 1853: 'Come we at last to the precipitous wooden steps by which we are to be mast-headed at a railway station. Good night to rosy-face, the cheeriest man we know, and up. Station very gritty, as a general characteristic. Station very dark, the gas being frozen. Station very cold, as any timber cabin suspended in the air with such a wind making lunges at it, would be.'**
Author's collection

Above: **High Level station occupies a large area and originally included its own goods station, known as Mill Street. This imposing structure included four warehouses and its own integral canal basins with four loading faces. Here, a DMU arrives at High Level with the 12.15 service from Walsall, as Class 5MT No 44715 of 1934 waits with a Birmingham-bound express on 13 April 1963.** *Bryan Jennings*

Centre left: **As originally built, both of Wolverhampton's railway stations had overall roofs. That over High Level survived the longest, being dropped onto the rails and platforms in one day — 22 February 1965 — which required closure of the station. Something of what was lost that day can be seen in this view of the interior of High Level station taken in the early 1960s.** *Author's collection*

Bottom left: **More features of the original High Level station and its overall roof can be seen in this early-1960s view of an express from Manchester and Liverpool to Birmingham New Street departing behind Class 5MTs Nos 45310 and 44715.** *Bryan Jennings*

Right: **Wolverhampton Low Level station took so long to build that it was not completed in time for the opening of either of the lines that used it. When the OWW opened on 1 July 1854 and the BW&D on 14 November 1854 the station was still a building site, and it probably remained so until the end of 1855. This 1906 view shows the station's extended frontage and its overall glass roof, which was its dominant feature until removed in stages between October 1933 and May 1934. On the far right can be glimpsed some of the buses that worked the Bridgnorth service, introduced on 7 November 1904.** *Author's collection*

Below: **The first of a series of photographs depicting a run into Wolverhampton Low Level along the OWW line. Facilities at stations along this line were a little basic. This is Princes End & Coseley in the early 1960s, with a large group waiting on the platform opposite a Stourbridge local train.** *Michael Mensing*

Bottom left: **Possibly the group in the previous photograph were waiting for an excursion special, such as the return one 'Modified Hall' No 7904** *Fountains Hall* **brought into Princes End & Coseley on Whit Monday — 11 June — 1961. One of the wooden shelters provided for passengers' 'comfort' can be seen above the first carriage. Passenger services along the OWW line were withdrawn on 30 July 1962.** *Michael Mensing*

Bottom right: **The next station on from Princes End & Coseley towards Wolverhampton Low Level was Daisy Bank & Bradley. On 30 July 1961 — exactly a year before passenger services along the line were withdrawn — '5101' 2-6-2 tank No 4104 of 1929 pulls out of the station with the 14.45 Stourbridge Junction–Wolverhampton Low Level service.** *Michael Mensing*

Left: **Bilston's name was associated with no fewer than three stations — two on former GWR lines and one on the Stour Valley line. This is Bilston West, the last station before Priestfield, on the OWW line. On the evidence of this photograph it was a well-kept station, with tended flowerbeds and clean platforms. None of this good housekeeping counted for much though, as the station closed with the others on the line on 30 July 1962.** *Wolverhampton Library*

Centre left: **Approaching Wolverhampton Low Level, the OWW and BW&D lines joined at Priestfield. In this view of the station on 30 April 1960, '51xx' 2-6-2 tank No 5151 pulls the 17.27 Stourbridge Junction–Wolverhampton Low Level service away off the OWW line, with the BW&D line curving in from the left. The OWW was closed to all traffic on 1 January 1968 and taken out of use on 22 September that year, but the BW&D half of Priestfield remained open for Birmingham Snow Hill–Wolverhampton Low Level services until conductor-guards were introduced on 5 May 1969.** *Michael Mensing*

Below: **The interior view of Low Level station with which people who knew it will be familiar. Following removal of its overall roof the station took on a much more open and airy feel. The camera is looking towards the double tunnel bringing the OWW lines into the station, seen to the right of the signalbox. Low Level has been caught in a quiet moment, at (if the clocks are to be believed) 5.35pm.** *Author's collection*

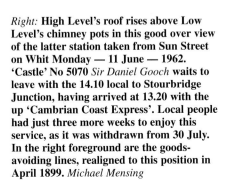

Above: **Trainspotters abound at the south end of Low Level station on 12 September 1959 as No 6861** *Crynant Grange* **comes off the 11.45 Birkenhead–Paddington service. The train was taken on to Paddington by No 6009** *King Charles II*. **This had been the pattern of Birkenhead express running until earlier in the year, when, following clearance tests with No 6011** *King James I* **on 13 April, 'Kings' were allowed to work through to Shrewsbury.** *Michael Mensing*

Right: **High Level's roof rises above Low Level's chimney pots in this good over view of the latter station taken from Sun Street on Whit Monday — 11 June — 1962. 'Castle' No 5070** *Sir Daniel Gooch* **waits to leave with the 14.10 local to Stourbridge Junction, having arrived at 13.20 with the up 'Cambrian Coast Express'. Local people had just three more weeks to enjoy this service, as it was withdrawn from 30 July. In the right foreground are the goods-avoiding lines, realigned to this position in April 1899.** *Michael Mensing*

Above: **The first of a series of photographs depicting a run out of Wolverhampton Low Level along the BW&D line. Approaching Priestfield station at Monmore Green, 4-4-0 No 3440** *City of Truro* **heads an SLS special to Swindon on 16 June 1957. The permanence of the railway infrastructure is illusory: within 10 years, traffic on this busy main line would be limited to local trains to/from Birmingham Snow Hill. The telegraph pole to the right of the Heinz Salad Cream poster is particularly impressive.** *Geoff Bannister*

Centre left: **After being mothballed following its closure in 1972, the BW&D line was revived in the late 1990s to form the route of Line 1 of the Midland Metro. Hub of the system is Wednesbury, where its main control centre and maintenance depot are based. Almost a century earlier,** *c*1902, **this was the scene at Wednesbury station, with an ex-West Midland Railway 2-4-0, GWR No 214, calling with a local service.** *Roger Carpenter collection*

Bottom left: **This second view of Wednesbury station** *c*1902, **possibly recorded on the same occasion, features a Dean Single storming through. The station buildings are lost in the smoke, but the gap between the lines reveals that this was once a mixed-gauge line, with both broad- and standard-gauge tracks laid between the platforms.** *Roger Carpenter collection*

Right: **Seemingly little changed at Wednesbury station between *c*1902 and March 1966, when this view towards Wolverhampton was recorded. By this time the extra space between the tracks had been put to good use, to accommodate signal wire and point roding. A train has clearly just departed as three passengers are heading towards the exit. In the distance can be seen the imposing works of the Patent Shaft & Axletree Co.** *Andrew Muckley*

Centre right: **Taken on the same occasion in March 1966 was this photograph of a Wellington-bound DMU entering Wednesbury station. Much of the original station detail had survived, most notably the footbridge. Sadly, from 5 May 1969 Wednesbury became an unstaffed halt, and the last passenger train called there on 4 March 1972.** *Andrew Muckley*

Bottom right: **On 1 September 1866 the GWR opened a link between the BW&D line and Dudley. This left the BW&D just past Swan Village station and provided GWR passengers at Dudley with a direct route to Birmingham. The junction of this line can be seen to good effect in this June 1957 view of No 5932 *Haydon Hall* working a Bournemouth–Wolverhampton express past Swan Village.** *IAL*

Left: **DMUs were introduced on Western Region Black Country services from 17 June 1957. Here a pair of three-car Swindon cross-country DMU sets form the 09.30 Birmingham–Cardiff service, seen approaching Swan Village on 26 April 1964. The tunnel-back houses seen at right were a characteristic part of the Black Country railway scene, especially to the east of Dudley towards Birmingham.** *Michael Mensing*

Centre left: **By the late 1950s the original Swan Village station, a timber structure, was showing its age, and around 1958 it was replaced with the modern single-storey building seen at left. All that remained from the original station was the footbridge. Here, during 1966, a pannier-hauled coal train heads through the station away from Wolverhampton.** *Roger Carpenter collection*

Below: **The gradient at Swan Village station is emphasised in this view taken in March 1966. A motor parcels van, probably Gloucester-built, has just passed over the level crossing, whose gates are still closed, barring traffic from crossing the railway.** *Andrew Muckley*

Right: **In part the BW&D line was protected after closure in 1972 by being used as a cycle route. Part of the reinstatement of the line for the Midland Metro required the building of a new cycle route alongside the Metro tracks, so this scene, with its sinuous curves and engineering-brick retaining wall, is once more a familiar one to Metro users and cyclists. On 3 August 1957, however, a three-car Birmingham suburban DMU set was climbing away from Swan Village with the 14.10 Wellington–Lapworth service.**
Michael Mensing

Left: **There appears to be a line of wagons on a siding just the other side of the road bridge as a three-car suburban DMU set forming the 14.48 Lapworth–Wellington service heads away from West Bromwich on 16 September 1961. The rocky outcrop makes the scene appear quite dramatic, like something one might expect to see at the coast, not almost 100 miles inland!**
Michael Mensing

Right: **All of the main BW&D stations had a similar appearance. Compare this view of West Bromwich station with the earlier ones of Wednesbury. A Birmingham-bound DMU set has arrived at West Bromwich in March 1966 as the camera looks back towards Wolverhampton.** *Andrew Muckley*

Left: **Churchward-designed '28xx' 2-8-0 No 2811 was 55 years old when photographed hauling a down part-fitted freight into West Bromwich station on 17 September 1958 — the author's fourth birthday! Much detail has been captured in this shot, especially the wooden lineside hut to the left, complete with trestle and large paraffin can. To the right is evidence of track realignment.** *Michael Mensing*

Below: **A different camera angle has made West Bromwich station appear much more enclosed in this view of No 6862 *Derwent Grange* arriving with the 17.20 Wolverhampton–Paddington service on 12 September 1958. The more modern shelter at left is in marked contrast to the rest of the Victorian station buildings and paraphernalia.** *Michael Mensing*

Left: **A link was made between the BW&D and Stourbridge Extension lines by a line that opened on 1 April 1867 between Smethwick and Handsworth junctions. A halt was opened near to the latter junction on 25 December 1931 to serve The Hawthorns, the ground of West Bromwich Albion FC. On 25 March 1961 a three-car suburban DMU set, forming the 13.30 Bewdley–Birmingham Snow Hill service, passes The Hawthorns Halt. The photographer is standing on the down Stourbridge platform.** *Michael Mensing*

Right: **One reason for being at The Hawthorns Halt on 25 March 1961 was that West Bromwich Albion were playing Everton, and a number of excursion specials called there. Here '51xx' 2-6-2T No 4173 works the empty stock from one of these excursions away.** *Michael Mensing*

Below: **Also on 25 March 1961, Class 5MT No 44907 pulls away from The Hawthorns Halt after depositing its train load of Everton supporters, the last of whom can be seen silhouetted against the skyline on Halford Lane. The signalbox, glimpsed through the bridge, controlled access to and from the Stourbridge line.** *Michael Mensing*

Right: **Another of the imposing BW&D line stations was that at Handsworth & Smethwick. In this track-level shot a two-car DMU set is about to depart on a service to Dudley, via the link line at Swan Village.** *R. C. Riley*

Left: **A solitary figure gives some scale to this March 1966 view of Handsworth & Smethwick station, looking towards Birmingham.** *Andrew Muckley*

Below: **Hockley station is arguably a bit 'off the coal' as far as the Black Country is concerned, but, like Soho & Winson Green, it was rarely photographed. This is the entrance, which was on the corner of Inknield Street and Park Road, photographed on 24 April 1964. There seems to be a car door leaning against the back wall!** *Ron Moss*

Above : **Originally called plain Soho, Soho & Winson Green station gained its longer and more familiar name in May 1893. The main station building was on Benson Road and was rarely photographed, making this May 1964 view all the more valuable.** *Ron Moss*

Below: **When the frontage of Low Level station was photographed after a shower on 22 September 1984, hopes were high that the station, which had closed as a Parcels Concentration Depot on 12 June 1981, would be saved and found a new use.** *Author*

Above: **The availability of labour under the Manpower Services Commission (MSC) also allowed urgent building-repair work to be undertaken at Low Level, such as the rebuilding of the pediment in the main frontage, seen here from the inside in 1985. Through the round window can be glimpsed carriages at the High Level station.** *Author*

Above: **Another aspect of Stage 2 of the MSC works programme at Low Level station in 1985 involved removal of a partition installed by the GWR to divide the original booking hall into two. With this gone, the elegance of the original design was seen once more. The openings above and to the left of the table are where the original booking-office windows once were.** *Author*

Below: **Stage 2 of the MSC works programme saw elements of the station's interior repaired and included removal of 10in of concrete from the left-hand platform, added so that BR parcel trolleys could be loaded into wagons without the use of ramps. This view, also from 1985, shows that work underway.** *Author*

Above left: **Removal of the concrete from the main platform at Low Level station revealed two features — the original large stone flags and a bay platform that once accommodated trains to Wellington — both of which are seen here.** *Author*

Below: **Following publication of this author's earlier book,** *Rail Centres: Wolverhampton,* **a reader from Westport, Connecticut, very kindly sent in a copy of this photograph showing ex-GWR diesel railcar No 8 at Wolverhampton Low Level on 20 May 1951. The occasion was a railtour organised by Mick Smith and the Wolverhampton Locomotive Society. Of particular interest are the coaches, which are in the Wellington bay. Local railway historian Michael Hale can be seen standing in the centre of the group.** *Al Gwilliam*

Above right: **Perhaps the greatest discovery of all, right at the very end of the Wellington bay, was this short length of mixed-gauge track. The GWR's Black Country services had all been worked exclusively on the 'narrow' (standard) gauge from 1 April 1869, so this was indeed a remarkable find. Also, it is probably the only original broad-gauge track still** *in situ* **anywhere! Wolverhampton Low Level was listed Grade II on 25 March 1986. All work on the site ceased at about the same time, and the building stands, forlorn and neglected, apart from being the focus for occasional hare-brained schemes to convert it for inappropriate uses.** *Author*

Right: **Wolverhampton had many other railway delights. One it retains is Oxley Viaduct, at Bushbury. This has to pass over the Birmingham Canal, and it is worth looking at this photograph, taken about 100 years ago, for a moment in order to gain a full appreciation of the skill required to build it. Note also how the signal was mounted outside the parapet, to save space.** *Eric Hamilton collection*

Below left: **One of Wolverhampton's lost railway treasures was Wednesfield Road goods station, opened by the Midland Railway in 1881. Photographed in 1990, the building retained much of its original equipment, including its cranes. The author was instrumental in getting the building listed, but, sadly, it was subsequently de-listed, and the site was redeveloped for a Post Office depot.** *Author*

Above right: **The LNWR began working into Chillington Basin on 10 September 1902. This provided a trans-shipment facility with the Birmingham Canal in basins beneath the canopy seen at the centre. This view was taken in 1990.** *Guy Sunbeam*

Left: **Although the canal basins at Chillington Basin have not been used for many years they remain in water, and the railway tracks are used as a siding by Wolverhampton Steel Terminal, which, in part, also serves a nearby British Oxygen depot.** *Guy Sunbeam*

3. WALSALL

Walsall has a railway history as long and complicated as Wolverhampton's, but one largely unresearched by historians. As with Wolverhampton, Walsall was 'served' by the GJR line from 4 July 1837. The station, the first of six to serve the town, was at Bescot Bridge, not exactly convenient for the town centre!

Walsall owed its eminence as a railway town to John Robinson McClean, engineer to the South Staffordshire Railway (SSR). In addition to superintending the line's construction, McClean leased and operated it for 11 years, between 1850 and 1861. The first part of the SSR — essentially a northeast–southwest line through Walsall — opened between Bescot and a temporary station in Bridgeman Place, Walsall, on 1 November 1847. This was continued north, to a junction with the Midland at Winchor, on 9 April 1849. With this new line came a new station in Station Street, Walsall, which served the town between 9 April 1849 and 31 December 1883. In later years the 17¼-mile line through Brownhills proved a useful diversion route, and its closure, after last use by two football specials taking Walsall FC supporters to Rotherham on 18 January 1984, was regretted almost immediately.

South of Walsall the SSR opened to Dudley on 1 November 1849, although this was strictly a technicality, one train being run along contractors' track to fulfil the powers in the company's Act. Passenger services did not begin until 1 May 1850 and continued until withdrawal on 6 July 1964. Completing the SSR in McClean's time, the company opened a line from Ryecroft Junction, north of Walsall, to Cannock on 1 February 1858. The Cannock Mineral Railway, opened on 7 November 1859, extended this north to a junction with the Trent Valley line at Rugeley. On 1 February 1861 McClean's lease of the SSR was transferred to the LNWR, and the company was formally vested in the latter on 15 July 1867.

Following its purchase of the WWR on 1 July 1876, the Midland Railway connected it with its main line east of Birmingham by constructing the Wolverhampton, Walsall & Midland Junction Railway (WW&MJR) — effectively a continuation of the WWR to a junction with the Midland at Castle Bromwich. The WW&MJR opened to passengers on 1 July 1879. Joint use of Walsall station by the LNWR and the Midland also began at this time. By the early 1880s the station in Station Street was inadequate to cope with the increased numbers of passengers, so a new station was built in Park Street, which opened on 1 January 1884. Services on the WW&MJ continued until 18 January 1965.

The LNWR opened the Walsall Junction and Wolverhampton Junction railways — two mile-long link lines between the SSR and its GJ line south of Walsall — on 1 October 1881. Only the Walsall Junction line had an intermediate station, at Pleck, which, although closed temporarily between 1917 and 1924, remained open until 17 November 1958. Effectively completing Walsall's railways was the Walsall Wood branch, opened by the Midland on 1 April 1882. This lost its passenger services on 31 March 1930 but remained open to goods until 3 September 1962.

In the early 1880s the LNWR began to develop marshalling facilities at Bescot. An up yard came into use there on 1 December 1881, followed by new sorting sidings on 17 October 1892. In the mid-1960s Bescot Yard was rebuilt, the new arrangements coming into use on 18 April 1966.

Park Street station was damaged by fire on 1 April 1916. Wartime restrictions on labour and materials delayed its rebuilding, and a 'temporary' entrance was formed from Bradford Place — an arrangement that lasted for seven years! A rebuilt Park Street station opened on 10 November 1923 and served Walsall until it was demolished between August and October 1978 to make way for the Saddlers Centre; this incorporated a new station and was opened officially on 18 July 1980.

Left: **The first station to serve Walsall was at Bescot Bridge, on the Grand Junction Railway. Departmental unit No DB975042 is in the general vicinity of this station as it skirts the M6 on an approach to Bescot Yard, after a trip from Wolverhampton on 16 January 1975. The face of some Black Country railways was changed irrevocably by the construction of the M5 and M6 motorways in the 1960s. This is most noticeable around Walsall, where, in addition to scenes like this, the existence of the Wolverhampton & Walsall Railway as a through route was ended on 28 September 1964, when the trackbed was breached by motorway construction work.**
Philip D. Hawkins

Above: **The LNWR began to develop marshalling facilities at Bescot in the early 1880s, the up yard coming into use on 1 December 1881, followed by new sorting sidings on 17 October 1892. Bescot Yard was rebuilt in the mid-1960s, with the new arrangements coming into use there on 18 April 1966. Here, on 17 March 1962, '8F' No 48733 comes off the Walsall line at Bescot with a southbound freight. On the right, '8F' No 48766 is going on shed.**
Michael Mensing

Centre right: **DMUs first appeared on Black Country services with their introduction on the Birmingham–Lichfield service through Walsall on 5 March 1956. Units M56156 and M50401 are seen new at Walsall station in 1956, in a view looking over towards the town's Art School.**
Roger Carpenter collection

Bottom right: **Other London Midland Black Country services had to wait a further 2½ years — until 17 November 1958 — before DMUs were introduced. By 30 May 1959, however, when this two-car Park Royal set was photographed arriving at Walsall station as the 17.18 service from Dudley, they were a familiar part of the local railway scene.** *Michael Mensing*

Left: **Walsall's most enduring station fronted onto Park Street. Opened by the LNWR on 1 January 1884, it was damaged by fire on 1 April 1916, and wartime restrictions on materials and labour delayed its rebuilding. A rebuilt Park Street station was reopened on 10 November 1923. This 1950s view shows the exterior; particularly elegant is the glass and iron *porte-cochère*. The group of men on the right are perhaps waiting for one of Walsall's many trolleybuses.** *IAL*

Centre left: **Behind the *porte-cochère*, Park Street station's booking hall was cavernous. It had a bow end, with doors leading down to the platforms, which can be seen in the previous photograph. The work of architect H. J. Davis, the hall was made light and airy by skylights. Here, two passengers ignore each other amid a forest of posters exhorting travellers to send their 'Luggage in Advance' or warning them of a 'Revision of Fares'. The station was demolished between August and October 1978 for the Saddlers Centre, which incorporated a new station and was opened formally on 18 July 1980.** *IAL*

Bottom left: **The Walsall Wood branch was opened by the Midland Railway on 1 April 1882. Always a likely victim of service cutbacks, it lost its passenger services from 31 March 1930. Walsall Wood station remained open to coal and goods traffic, which sustained the branch for the next 25 years, but from the late 1950s the branch was shortened progressively as collieries went out of use; ¾-mile closed from 23 March 1957, a further stretch going from 3 June 1962. Three months later, on 3 September 1962, the remaining facilities at Walsall Wood station were withdrawn, and the branch closed completely.** *IAL*

4. DUDLEY

Dudley's first rail services were provided by the SSR, when its southern extension finally opened on 1 May 1850, with intermediate stations at Wednesbury, Great Bridge and Dudley Port. This was to a temporary station at the foot of Castle Hill, where, later, a joint station was built with the OWW. The latter opened its line between Stourbridge and Dudley to passengers on 20 December 1852, with intermediate stations at Brettell Lane, Brierley Hill & Round Oak and Netherton. This was extended to Tipton on 1 December 1853, including a junction with the LNWR's Stour Valley line, known as the Tipton Curve. One month later, on 2 January 1854, a second connection was made to the Stour Valley line when the SSR opened a link spur between the two lines just south of Dudley Port station; this also gave the LNWR access to Dudley. The OWW completed its line to Wolverhampton on 1 July 1854 by opening between Tipton and Priestfield, the latter being the junction with the BWD.

Thus Dudley was well connected with Wolverhampton and Walsall, but lacked a direct link to Birmingham. This was rectified from 1 September 1866 with the opening of a line between the BWD at Swan Village and the SSR just north of Dudley Port station, with an intermediate station at Great Bridge. A second link to Birmingham came on 1 March 1878, when a line was opened between Old Hill and a new station called Dudley (South Side) & Netherton on the OWW, just south of Dudley Tunnel.

For most of its working life Dudley station was a joint one between the LNWR (later LMS) and the GWR. Facilities were not so much shared as replicated, and the station was effectively two, co-existing side-by-side.

Services on the OWW line were withdrawn from 30 July 1962, and those to and from Old Hill last ran on 13 June 1964. This just left those to Walsall along the SSR, which survived a further three weeks; thus Dudley closed to passengers on 6 July 1964, although the station remained open for parcels until August 1966. Demolition work to clear the station site began in January 1967, and throughout the year it was transformed into a Freightliner depot — the first train departing on 6 November 1967. This sustained railway activity at Dudley for 19 years, the last Freightliner train departing at 18.45 on 29 September 1986. However, freight trains continued to trundle through the station site using a hybrid route comprising the OWW's southern approach and the SSR's northern exit; the last train to use this ran on 22 March 1993. In 2003 the route was due to be utilised by Line 3 of the Midland Metro, between Wednesbury and Brierley Hill, but this is planned to avoid the former station site by running up Castle Hill into Dudley bus station.

Below: **At various times the products of one of Wednesbury's largest firms were to be found all over the railway network. The Patent Shaft & Axletree Co was founded in 1835 to make and improve axles for carts, and from 1853 its output included the production of railway wheels. On 18 April 1902 the company became part of a new company, the Metropolitan Amalgamated Railway Carriage & Wagon Co Ltd, which eventually became Metro-Cammell. This view inside the wheel-lathe shop dates from around the time of the amalgamation in 1902. The din from the belt-driven machinery must have been tremendous!** *Author*

Above left: **The start of a journey to Dudley along the South Staffordshire line. This view, looking north at Wednesbury Town station, was recorded in March 1966, almost two years after it had closed to passengers. Branching off to the left is the Darlaston Loop, opened on 14 September 1863, with an intermediate station at Darlaston; this fell victim to competition from steam trams and lost its passenger service from 1 November 1887. Leaking steam and producing clouds of black smoke, Stanier '8F' No 48526 works a mixed freight through the closed station.** *Andrew Muckley*

Bottom left: **Seen from the same vantage point — Potter's Lane Bridge — on 20 August 1963, a Park Royal DMU set pulls away from Wednesbury Town with a Dudley service. This view also shows the bay platform to the right, from where trains on the Princes End branch used to leave. This opened on the same day as the Darlaston Loop and connected with the Stour Valley Line at Bloomfield Junction, via Ocker Hill and Princes End. Another unprofitable line, it was eventually closed to passengers on 1 January 1916.** *M.J. Fox*

Above right: **At Great Bridge, in addition to a passenger station, the LNWR/LMS had extensive goods facilities. These are seen in the mid-1930s on the occasion of the commissioning of a new 25-ton electric overhead-gantry crane, which dominates this view. Great Bridge also had facilities for canal trans-shipment.** *IAL*

Centre right: **Apart from a substantial brick building, whose chimneys can just be glimpsed to the right, most facilities at Dudley Port (Low Level) were timber-built. An exception is the modern flat-roofed waiting room, seen here to the left of the leading cab of a two-car Park Royal DMU set leaving on the 17.18 Dudley– Walsall service on 25 July 1959. Above, on Dudley Port High Level station, on the Stour Valley line, a boy stares back at the camera.** *Michael Mensing*

Bottom right: **Between Dudley Port (Low Level) and Dudley the South Staffordshire line crossed fairly level ground. A two-car Park Royal DMU set, forming the 16.18 Dudley–Walsall service, approaches Dudley Port (Low Level) on 25 July 1959. To the left, two vans and a wagon stand in the siding used by Palethorpes for traffic to and from that firm's nearby sausage works. To the right is the sweep of the embankment that carried the link spur between the SSR and Stour Valley lines, which came into use on 2 January 1854.** *Michael Mensing*

Left: **This seemingly ordinary photograph is in fact a record of a piece of history. It shows the last scheduled passenger train, the 20.10, leaving Dudley station along the SSR *en route* to Birmingham Snow Hill on 14 July 1964. The train was a hybrid six-car suburban DMU formation, headed by single car No 55018. The grassed-over tracks to the right indicate the site of the former LNWR/LMS goods yard; the building on top of the brick-arched caverns was the goods office fronting onto Tipton Road.** *Michael Mensing*

Below: **Tipton Road also provided a good vantage point from which to photograph the northern end of Dudley station. Dudley East signalbox controlled access to the SSR and the former LNWR/LMS goods yard seen in the previous photograph. The skyline is dominated by the fly tower of Dudley Hippodrome, which replaced the town's opera house, destroyed by fire in 1936. At Easter 1961, '5MT' 2-6-0 No 42823 hauls a return excursion onto the SSR from Dudley, *en route* to Derby.** *IAL*

Left: **Recorded three years later from the same vantage point, this view of a two-car Park Royal DMU set leaving Dudley with the 17.18 local to Walsall on 2 May 1964 also shows much incidental detail, including lorries on the sloping Station Drive and the parcels depot above.** *Michael Mensing*

Above: **We now journey along the OWW to Dudley, where Parkhead Viaduct carried the line over a complicated series of canal junctions. As with other GWR viaducts in the Black Country, Parkhead was first built as a timber structure but was replaced in the 1880s by a brick one, as seen here in February 1966. The cottage to the left was provided for the lock-keeper, while the building to the right is a pump house erected in 1893/4 to overcome water loss associated with the operation of Parkhead locks.** *Andrew Muckley*

Right: **Blowers Green station was served by trains from both OWW and Old Hill lines. It was opened with the Old Hill line on 1 March 1878 as Dudley Southside & Netherton, but was renamed Blowers Green from 1 August 1921. By 1955, when this view was recorded of '61xx' 2-6-2T No 6118 working a goods train through the station, the buildings were in a very run-down state, and the booking office had been replaced by a new structure on New Road. Behind is the southern portal of the tunnel leading to Dudley station.**
W.R. Lait/Dudley Libraries

Above: **Dudley from the air in the 1950s. A large extension is being added to the Technical College in the foreground. Above this, rising through the trees, is Dudley Castle and Zoo. The two halves of Dudley station can be seen at the top. The lower portion with the shorter canopy, was the ex-GWR side, the upper portion being the ex-LMS one. Tipton Road crosses the picture horizontally, and the SSR can be seen curving under this on the left. The building below this point was the Western Region's Castle Goods, whilst that on the extreme left was London Midland Region's Town Goods.** *Aerofilms*

Left: **The view across Dudley station from the GWR platform, *c*1903. 0-6-0ST No 1513 is coupled to a wagon belonging to M. & W. Grazebrook Ltd, whose collieries and furnaces were at Parkhead in Netherton. On the right stands an LNWR coach, whilst above is the best known view of the Dudley, Stourbridge & District Electric Tramways depot at the foot of Castle Hill. This had two roads inside and one down the outside, on which two trams are parked.** *Roger Carpenter collection*

Right: **The platform in the previous photograph is now in the foreground in this view from Castle Hill Road bridge, recorded in the early 1950s. Nearest the camera is Dudley South signalbox, which projected from the end of the platform; by this time its lower half had been strengthened with a formidable brick skirt. A pannier tank rests in a bay platform on the ex-GWR side, while the ex-LMS platform to the right is alive with passengers.** *Roger Carpenter collection*

Below: **A view from one of the windows in the ex-GWR station building at Dudley in January 1956, looking back towards the Castle Hill Road bridge, from where the previous photograph was taken. A carriage occupies the bay platform. The remarkable 'TV picture' shape of the large bridge opening is shown to good effect. Beyond is a water tank.** *Dudley Libraries*

Bottom left: **Now-preserved 2-6-2T No 4555 has arrived at Dudley with an SLS special on 13 June 1964, behind the last regular passenger service along the Old Hill line. She is the object of much interest as enthusiasts and photographers record what they can of Dudley's rapidly vanishing railway life.** *Ron Moss*

Bottom right: **Dudley station closed to passengers on 6 July 1964. It remained open for parcels until August 1966, but in January 1967 work began to clear the site, and during the year it was transformed into a Freightliner depot, from which the first train would depart on 6 November 1967. This use sustained railway activity at Dudley for 19 years, the last Freightliner train departing at 18.45 on 29 September 1986, but freight trains continued to trundle through the station site until 22 March 1993.** *Neil Pitts/Author's collection*

5. STOURBRIDGE

The OWW opened its passenger services northwards towards Wolverhampton in nine stages, those between Droitwich and Stourbridge commencing on 3 May 1852. The station was called simply 'Stourbridge', gaining its more familiar 'Junction' tag when a new branch to Stourbridge Town opened on 1 October 1879. This soon highlighted the inadequacy of the original station accommodation at Stourbridge Junction. An enlarged station was the answer, but the site was 'rail-locked', so the original station was endured for 15 or so years until the GWR proposed to build a new Junction station ¼ mile south. This came into use on 1 October 1901, with a realigned town branch.

The OWW opened a single branch line to Oak Farm Colliery on 14 November 1858. This left the main line just north of Brettell Lane station at Kingswinford Junction. By 1860 the Askew Bridge branch extended the line to Himley Colliery. In the early 20th century this was further extended to serve a new colliery at Baggeridge. At the same time the GWR proposed extending the Kingswinford branch as part of an ambitious scheme to connect Stourbridge and Wolverhampton by rail with Bridgnorth. The line was to be doubled and extended through Wombourne and Tettenhall to join the S&B at Oxley. Construction was delayed until late 1913 and abandoned in 1916 through labour and materials shortages. Work resumed in 1921, and the line opened on 11 January 1925. A steam railmotor service between Stourbridge Junction and Wolverhampton, with halts at Brockmoor, Bromley, Pensnett, Gornal, Himley, a station at Wombourne, halts at Penn and Compton and a station at Tettenhall, commenced on 11 May 1925, but low passenger numbers saw this withdrawn on 31 October 1932 and the halts closed. The route proved a useful engineering diversion, and both stations remained open for goods until 6 July 1964, but the line closed on 1 March 1965. Baggeridge Colliery closed on 1 March 1968 and all the lines serving it from north of Shutt End were closed on 1 April 1968.

The GWR built an engine shed at Stourbridge in 1870, ½ mile north of Stourbridge station, off the OWW line on the far side of Stambermill Viaduct. It could hold 20 locomotives and also had a coaling stage and 45ft-diameter turntable. A 28-road roundhouse, with 65ft-diameter turntable, which came into use on 8 February 1926, superseded these facilities. This was the last roundhouse built by the GWR. A DMU-refuelling point was installed in 1956. The shed closed to steam on 11 July 1966 but continued to house DMUs until 6 May 1968. Both sheds were demolished by June 1969.

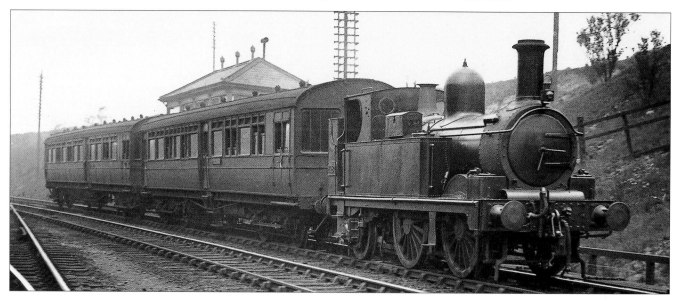

Above: **A GWR 0-4-2T, possibly No 148, has been checked at Stourbridge in the late 1920s with its short train comprising a pair of auto-trailers, probably for use on the Stourbridge Town branch.** *IAL*

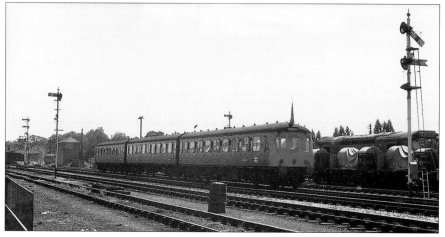

Bottom left: **A three-car DMU set — plus a diesel locomotive and some cable drum wagons — stabled in the sidings at Stourbridge Junction in July 1970. To the left is the Middle signalbox, while on the extreme left are the canopies of the main station.** *Neil Pitts/Author's collection*

Right: **Stourbridge's original station opened with the commencement of the OWW's services from Droitwich on 3 May 1852. The opening of a new branch into Stourbridge Town on 1 October 1879, plus a general increase in traffic, meant that by the end of the 19th century the original buildings were both life-expired and in the wrong place. Thus was built a new station, ¼ mile south of the original, which came into use, with a realigned Town branch, on 1 October 1901. How other than this could any self-respecting Stourbridge resident send their Christmas greetings that year? A century on, Chawn Hill (behind the station) is entirely built upon.** *Brian Standish*

Left: **Platform 4 at Stourbridge Junction, from a postcard postmarked 1903. Lots of heads and arms are out of the carriage windows, and the train is moving off in the direction of Kidderminster. By her posture, the lady in the white skirt is probably taking a photograph. The occasion is unknown, but it may have been an outing of some kind. In 2003 this platform has only cars parked against it.** *Brian Standish*

Right: **The relocation of Stourbridge Junction moved it from the end of Junction Road, to off Brook Road, where, in its wake, further building followed. The Seven Stars might as well have been the Station Hotel, as it stands directly opposite the end of the new Junction's carriage drive. Little altered in 2003, it features a clubroom upstairs; *c*1905 the landlord stands proudly on his step, with his dog.** *Brian Standish*

Above left: **Two views of Stourbridge Junction from November 1967. Platforms 3 and 4 are viewed from Platform 2. The new station consisted of a pair of island platforms with largely duplicate facilities on each.** *Neil Pitts/Author's collection*

Above right: **An overview of Stourbridge Junction in November 1967, from Chawn Hill. The view is across from Platform 4 to Platform 1. There is an air of neglect and abandonment that belies the bright future Stourbridge Junction was to enjoy in the decades ahead.** *Neil Pitts/Author's collection*

Below left: **Stourbridge Junction was extensively modernised in the late 1980s. Some of the platform buildings were thinned, especially those on Platforms 3 and 4, and the canopies were cut back. The old entrance building was also replaced. Here is the original building, recorded in March 1988, just prior to demolition.** *Neil Pitts/Author's collection*

Below right: **This was the scene at Stourbridge Junction later in March 1988 when the original entrance building had been demolished and work had begun on the erection of its replacement.** *Neil Pitts/Author's collection*

Left: **Passing through Stourbridge Junction — 1. Over the years Stourbridge Junction has formed part of the route of many railway excursions and specials. Here, on 17 October 1965, 0-6-2T No 6667 takes water on an SLS special to Bristol, whilst a 'classic' schoolboy moves forward to capture the scene on his camera. The author means no disrespect by that last remark — he too had to dress like that once!** *Andrew Muckley*

Right: **Passing through Stourbridge Junction — 2. GWR 2-4-0T No 976 pulls away from Platform 3 at Stourbridge Junction with an up Kidderminster service in the 1920s. The tracks to the right came from Platform 4 and carriage sidings situated beyond this, whilst the point rods led from Stourbridge South signalbox, which was just behind the photographer.** *IAL*

Centre right: **Passing through Stourbridge Junction — 3. The southern approach to Stourbridge Junction remains pleasantly rural but was more so in the 1920s, when this view of a GWR 0-4-2T approaching from Hagley was recorded. The bridge behind carries Hagley Road over the railway.** *IAL*

Below: **Hagley is the next station south from Stourbridge Junction. By no stretch of the imagination could it be classed as being in the Black Country, but its rural charm, epitomised by this postcard view, postmarked 1 October 1906, serves to emphasise the true nature of the area. This was industry in countryside, which it blackened by its smoke — black country. Hagley station also had some quintessential GWR elements, so much so that Hornby used the footbridge as the basis of its model of the same.** *Brian Standish*

Left: **A journey from Stourbridge Junction north along the OWW line. Few rivers were more heavily industrialised than the River Stour. In five miles between Halesowen and Stourbridge, no fewer than 42 forges, furnaces and mills made use of the river for water power. The same river had also to be culverted and bridged, and this was how the OWW crossed the Stour at Stambermill in the early 1850s. Photographed in 1865, the Brunelian timber viaduct looks down on breeze ovens and other evidence of small-scale industrial activity.** *Dudley Libraries*

Above: **The timber viaduct at Stambermill was replaced by the brick structure that still stands in 2003. This work was achieved between 20 September 1881 and 14 April 1882, coming into use on 10 May 1882. The new viaduct was built slightly to the west of the original, one of the brick bases from which can be seen on the right of this view of a freight train crossing in March 1966.** *Andrew Muckley*

Bottom left: **Just the other side of Stambermill Viaduct was Stourbridge engine shed. Stourbridge Engine Shed signalbox, seen here in March 1968, controlled movements into and out of the shed, plus five through sidings. This 'box outlasted the shed, and finally closed on 11 May 1969.** *Neil Pitts/Author's collection*

Above left: **The original engine shed at Stourbridge was constructed in 1870. Plans for its expansion were shelved due to the Great War but were revived when the project was seen as one suitable for funding as part of a Government Unemployment Relief Scheme in the mid-1920s. These plans included the coaling stage, the rear of which is seen here in March 1968, almost two years after the shed had closed.** *Neil Pitts/Author's collection*

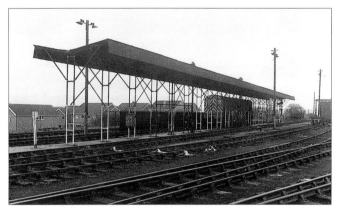

Above right: **On top of the coaling stage at Stourbridge engine shed was a 75,000-gallon water tank, seen here from the front, again in March 1968. The actual coaling apparatus can be seen protruding from the stage at first-floor height.** *Neil Pitts/Author's collection*

Centre right: **DMUs were introduced on the Western Region's Black Country local train services on 17 June 1957, and in preparation for this a diesel fuelling stage was installed at Stourbridge engine shed.** *Neil Pitts/Author's collection*

Right: **When the new engine shed was opened at Stourbridge the old four-road shed, far from being closed or demolished, was retained and became a depot for steam railmotors, diesel railcars and, later, DMUs. For its latter usage the building was partly rebuilt, and it was in this form that it was photographed in March 1968.**
Neil Pitts/Author's collection

Above left: **Back in June 1953, when Stourbridge engine shed was still open, ex-GWR 2-6-2T No 5191 was photographed on the approach lines to the new shed. In the background a rake of wagons is stored on the through sidings.** *Neil Pitts/Author's collection*

Above right: **On the same occasion in June 1953, ex-GWR 2-6-2T No 5178 was photographed at Stourbridge engine shed, slightly closer to the new shed. More wagons can be glimpsed behind, whilst a large water tank stands atop an embankment.**
Neil Pitts/Author's collection

Left: **The approach to the new shed at Stourbridge in March 1968, with the end of the main building, and the chimneys from its two stationary boilers, just in view at the left.** *Neil Pitts/Author's collection*

Above: **In June 1953 ex-GWR 2-6-2T No 5165 was photographed on the approach to the new shed at Stourbridge, with the chimneys for stationary boilers seen on the end of the shed.** *Neil Pitts/Author's collection*

Bottom left: **A general view of the new shed at Stourbridge in March 1968. This took the form of a 28-road roundhouse, whose principal dimensions were 219ft by 255ft, based around a 65ft-diameter turntable. The roundhouse was built by Wollaston builder Harry Guest, and the whole scheme cost £119,230.** *Neil Pitts/Author's collection*

Left: **The two stationary boilers, recycled from scrapped locomotives, provided steam for power, heating and boiler washouts at Stourbridge engine shed. This close-up of these stationary boilers was taken in March 1968.**
Neil Pitts/Author's collection

Above right: **Sidings were provided alongside the roundhouse at Stourbridge engine shed. Ex-GWR 0-6-2T No 5651 was photographed on these tracks in June 1953.**
Neil Pitts/Author's collection

Below: **Inside the roundhouse at Stourbridge engine shed in March 1968, with a Mini providing a useful scale. The shed closed to steam on 11 July 1966, and all the buildings had been cleared by June 1969. In 2003 housing covers the site, arrayed along roads that carry the names of GWR Chief Mechanical Engineers and Locomotive Superintendents.** *Neil Pitts/Author's collection*

Above: **Further along the OWW line, just past the site of Brettell Lane station, is Kingswinford Junction, seen here in July 1968 from Moor Lane Bridge. This came into use on 14 November 1858 as the Kingswinford branch, a link to Bromley Basin on the Stourbridge Extension Canal. Ahead, off the main line, is Moor Lane Yard, which was subsequently developed into Brierley Hill Steel Terminal.** *Neil Pitts/Author's collection*

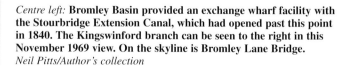

Centre left: **Bromley Basin provided an exchange wharf facility with the Stourbridge Extension Canal, which had opened past this point in 1840. The Kingswinford branch can be seen to the right in this November 1969 view. On the skyline is Bromley Lane Bridge.** *Neil Pitts/Author's collection*

Bottom left: **A close-up of the trans-shipment shed at Bromley Basin, also from November 1969. This was taken from a footbridge carrying the towpath over the canal, which is a recycled railway bridge, bearing the legend 'GWR Reading' in various places.** *Neil Pitts/Author's collection*

Above: **By 1984, when this view was recorded, the canal had been drained, but the railway remained open as far as Shutt End, where a road/rail depot had been set up for the distribution of bottled Perrier water. Ahead is Bromley Lane Road Bridge.** *Author*

Centre right: **Bromley Lane Bridge, seen in November 1924, when engineers from the South Staffordshire Waterworks Co were laying a water main along the parapet. The canal was still in use, and the railway was being prepared for its new passenger service, which commenced the following May.** *South Staffs Water*

Bottom right: **The GWR planned a new route from Stourbridge to Wolverhampton via Wombourne in 1908. Negotiations with the Earl of Dudley and the Great War delayed its completion until the early 1920s, when the GWR obtained Unemployment Relief Funding, as it did for Stourbridge engine shed, to complete the work. Most of the 'stations' were simple halts, with GWR-style pagodas, as seen here at Bromley Halt, in a rare photograph taken while it was open to passengers.** *Author's collection*

Above: **Operated by steam railmotors, the passenger service on the GWR's new line was not a great success, having to contend with bus competition, and was withdrawn on 31 October 1932. Amazingly,** **one of the pagodas at Bromley Halt survived a long time and was still there to be photographed in July 1968.** *Neil Pitts/Author's collection*

Above left: **Boring for coal at Baggeridge began in 1896, and the first shafts were sunk in 1899. Served initially by a narrow-gauge (2ft 6in) line, the new colliery was connected by standard-gauge lines both to the Pensnett Railway and to the GWR at Askew Bridge. These were constructed by the GWR but operated solely by Pensnett Railway locomotives and staff. Production began in 1912. At 15.50 on 17 October 1959, '8F' No 48430, working a down freight, leaves the double track for the single line at Baggeridge Junction.** *Author's collection*

Above right: **This is the same spot, looking in the opposite direction, at 15.00 on 5 February 1960. Baggeridge Colliery employed over 1,000 men underground and had a large output from the start. The author's grandfather worked there and was killed in an accident in 1934.** *Author's collection*

Left: **Ex-GWR 'Hall' No 4939** *Littleton Hall* **leaves the single line for double track at Baggeridge Junction at 15.20 on 5 February 1960. In September 1966 traffic had become so light between Baggeridge and Round Oak that the line between the two was closed. The NCB continued to operate the section between Baggeridge and Askew Bridge until the colliery closed down on 2 March 1968. Limited rail traffic continued for a month, the track being taken out of use on 1 April 1968.**
Author's collection

Above: **There were only two substantial stations on the GWR's new line through Wombourne to Wolverhampton — Tettenhall and Wombourne. The latter is seen here in 1925, from the unusual vantage point of the local watercourse, known as The Bratch.**

A dapper gent has noticed the camera but not the rudimentary bridge behind him, whilst a pair of swans take it inturn to bathe. How did the table get there, though? *Author's collection*

Above: **The start of the single track at Baggeridge Junction, looking towards Himley, on 5 February 1960. The Baggeridge line passed through a corner of Himley Park, and between 1928 and 1937 passenger trains, using coaches leased from the GWR, were run on August Bank Holidays to convey people from Brierley Hill to special fêtes held at Himley. The junction was originally double-track but had been singled by 1956, and the connection to the Pensnett Railway was removed by 1 July that year.** *Author's collection*

Below: **A postcard view from the footbridge seen in the photograph on the previous page. The 'Batch' name never really caught on, and in its brief working life the station was known as Wombourne. It all looks very new here, particularly the bases of the water tower stanchions. Two men and a dog (quite literally) look up to 'populate' a scene that was probably taken immediately prior to the station's opening in May 1925.**
Author's collection

Bratch Station, Wombourne.

Stourbridge Town

The OWW passes almost ¾ mile east of Stourbridge. Its 1845 Act allowed for a branch into the town, but this was never built. The following year the Birmingham, Wolverhampton & Stour Valley Railway proposed a 20-mile branch from its line at Smethwick to Stourport via Old Hill, Stourbridge and Kidderminster. Unfortunately, this part of the 'Stour Valley' scheme met with opposition and was dropped. Proposals for lines and branches to Stourbridge came and went in the late 1840s and throughout the 1850s, culminating in 1857 with one for a goods-only branch to leave the main OWW line north of Stambermill Viaduct and terminate by Stourbridge Canal basin in Lower High Street. This was to be worked by a stationary winding engine. The powers under which this was built stated it had to be open by 31 July 1859. Construction began in April 1859, and by 30 July it was sufficiently complete for an opening ceremony to take place, using a locomotive and four horses instead of the winding engine. The latter was incomplete and took almost two years to install.

The incline did not provide a passenger service, so within a few years there were more calls for a new branch line into Stourbridge. Eventually the GWR proposed a 1-mile branch from Stourbridge station, descending by a double line at 1 in 400 to a passenger station in Foster Street and then dropping steeply at 1 in 27 by a single line to a junction with the existing branch at the foot of the incline. Construction began in spring 1878, and the line opened to passengers on 1 October 1879, with goods services to a new shed at the canal basin commencing on 1 January 1880. The incline closed on the same date.

The original OWW station was renamed Stourbridge Junction, the new station in Foster Street taking the name Stourbridge. From then the branch passenger service intensified. Between January 1905 and October 1935 it was operated by GWR steam railmotors, and these were replaced first by diesel railcars and then by single-unit railcars in 1958.

The GWR began a Stourbridge–Clent–Bromsgrove motor-omnibus service from the forecourt of Stourbridge Town station on 13 February 1905. This was withdrawn on 5 August 1916 but was briefly reinstated in lieu of train services during the General Strike.

The branch passenger service has been withdrawn twice — as a wartime economy between 29 March 1915 and 3 March 1919 and in the General Strike between 7 May and 10 July 1926. The double-track upper section of the branch was altered in 1935 to make the down line passenger-only and the up goods-only, these alterations coming into effect on 25 August that year.

Use of Stourbridge Goods station declined in the early 1960s with the closure of sidings branching off it to serve local firms and the nearby town gasworks. The last train to leave the station departed on 30 April 1965, and all work officially ceased at the yard on 5 July 1965, although the line remained open until 20 September 1965. The track was lifted by October 1967.

Passenger services on the Town branch have long been under threat. Stourbridge Town station was unstaffed from July 1967, but the buildings stood until February 1979, when they were demolished to make way for a rebuilt bus station, the line being shortened by 3 chains (66yd) as a result. Remodelling of the bus station shortened the branch further in February 1994, but Stourbridge did at least get a proper station building as a result, this being opened on 25 April 1994.

Above: **A journey down the Stourbridge Town and Goods branches. Passenger services on the new Stourbridge Town branch began on 1 October 1879, with goods services on to a new shed at the canal basin commencing on 1 January 1880. In April 1975 single car M55004 heads two other cars at the extreme end of Platform 1 at Stourbridge Junction.** *Neil Pitts/Author's collection*

Left: **Between January 1905 and October 1935 the Stourbridge Town branch was operated by GWR steam railmotors. These were replaced first by GWR diesel railcars and then, in 1958, by BR single-unit railcars. This 'Bubble' has just arrived at Stourbridge Junction as the 16.27 ex Stourbridge Town.** *Steve Blackman*

Below: **The passenger service on the Stourbridge Town branch has been withdrawn twice — firstly, between 29 March 1915 and 3 March 1919, as a wartime economy, and again, between 7 May and 10 July 1926, due to the General Strike. Here, on 18 May 1981, branch perennial M55004 has just arrived at the Junction with the 14.00 service from Stourbridge Town.** *Les Bertram*

Above: **Les Bertram must have spent a day photographing the branch on 18 May 1981. Two and a half hours later M55004 arrives at Stourbridge Junction with the 16.29 service from Stourbridge Town. Stourbridge Middle signalbox can be seen on the extreme right.** *Les Bertram*

Below: **Seen from Platform 3 some 12 years earlier, on 15 March 1969, M55004 (again) curves away from Stourbridge Junction towards the Town station. Much steam paraphernalia still remains at the Junction, but not for long.** *Roger Crombleholme*

Left: **The middle section of the Stourbridge Town branch was rarely if ever photographed. The author's grandparents lived along this section of the line in Junction Road, and pannier tanks chugging up the branch constitute his earliest memories of steam. This view is from the Stourbridge Town footbridge in November 1967, when the line still had both tracks** *in situ.* **St John's Church Hall can be seen on the right.**
Neil Pitts/Author's collection

Right: **Looking the opposite way on the same occasion in November 1967 produced this view of Stourbridge Town station. By this date the line on to the Town Goods station had been lifted, and the bridge over Foster Street East had been removed two months earlier. As a child, the author found Town station disproportionately large for its purpose, with lots of creepy empty rooms.** *Neil Pitts/Author's collection*

Left: **By 15 March 1969 the parallel goods line had been lifted, but clearly quite recently, as M55004 works towards Stourbridge Junction.** *Roger Crombleholme*

Right: **By 4 August 1980 grass had reclaimed the former goods line, as is apparent from this photograph of a Class 122 single car, taken from the Parkfield Road bridge. The old Town station had been demolished two years earlier and replaced by the shelters seen behind the footbridge.** *J.G. Glover*

Below: **From the platform, Stourbridge Town had a very rural aspect — if you could ignore the houses in Parkfield Road opposite, that is! The elaborate decoration on the platform canopy is seen to good effect in this view of M55004 entering the station on 15 March 1969.**
Roger Crombleholme

Upper left: **The Town station footbridge provided an excellent vantage point from which to view or photograph it. Seen on the same date as in the previous photograph, M55004 is about to depart. By this time the station was unstaffed, tickets being issued on the train.** *Roger Crombleholme*

Bottom left: **The exterior of Stourbridge Town station in November 1967. This connected directly with the town's bus station, in the days when integrated public transport was so obvious that the term hadn't even been coined to describe it. In form, the Town station was like that at Ross-on-Wye and would influence the design of the Severn Valley Railway's Kidderminster station.**
Neil Pitts/Author's collection

Above right: **On 13 February 1905 the GWR commenced an omnibus service between Stourbridge Town station and Bromsgrove via Hagley and Clent. The service was worked by two Milnes-Daimler 24hp petrol-engined omnibuses which seated 36 — 20 on top and 16 'inside'. This scene is outside Stourbridge Town station in 1910.** *Dudley Libraries*

Centre right: **The GWR Stourbridge–Bromsgrove service was still quite new when this view was recorded for a postcard. The card is postmarked 20 July 1908, but the photograph must have been taken a year or two earlier. The bus is in Upper High Street — more or less at the point where Stourbridge's beloved Ring Road carved through in 1968.** *Brian Standish*

Above:
This ticket was issued to the author's grandfather on a GWR omnibus for a journey between Stourbridge and Pedmore School in 1916. The service was withdrawn on 5 August that year as a wartime economy but was not reinstated after the Armistice.
Author's collection

Bottom right: **A second postcard view, probably contemporary with the first, shows one of the GWR omnibuses in Clent. It must have been a nice day, as the upper deck seems quite popular. The sheep will have to hurry, though, or they'll miss the bus!**
Brian Standish

Above: **Stourbridge Town station was demolished and rebuilt in February 1979, when this photograph was taken. The canopy has gone and the platform is being extended.**
Neil Pitts/Author's collection

Below: **Demolition of the old Town station buildings at Stourbridge in February 1979. The new 'station' — the shelter to the left — is already in place.** *Neil Pitts/Author's collection*

Right: **Old and new Stourbridge Town stations in February 1979, seen from the station footbridge.**
Neil Pitts/Author's collection

Left: **When the new Stourbridge Town station was completed in February 1979, the Town branch had been shortened by 70 yards, and a substantial brick wall erected to screen it from the bus station.**
Neil Pitts/Author's collection

Right: **Nine years on, the new Stourbridge Town station had settled down, and memories of the old station had begun to fade. This was the scene on 18 March 1988, with 'bubble car' M55032 waiting to depart for Stourbridge Junction.** *Nigel Hunt*

Upper left: **By the early 1990s the need for an ever larger bus station saw the Stourbridge Town branch shortened by a further 30 yards and a new 170ft platform and booking office erected. This necessitated the temporary closure of the branch. The new station opened on 25 April 1994 and was opened officially on 3 May that year.** *Neil Pitts/Author's collection*

Bottom left: **The Stourbridge Town Canal Arm was extended under Lower High Street in the 1830s to serve Orme & Foster's Ironworks. In the late 1870s this area was redeveloped to provide a new goods shed and canal basin, to which goods services commenced on 1 January 1880. Stourbridge goods station isseen here in November 1967, following its closure.** *Neil Pitts/Author's collection*

Above right: **There was a spectacular crash at Stourbridge Town goods station on Easter Monday — 24 April — 1905, when a 32-wagon goods train ran away down the gradient, sending its leading banker through the buffer-stops, across 15ft of trackless yard and through both walls of the 20ft-wide goods office. A photographer from the local** *County Express* **newspaper recorded these views.** *Brian Standish*

Above: **The force of the impact on 24 April 1905 can be seen by the effect it had on the leading two wagons, which were forced up into this rather spectacular pyramid. Stourbridge's gasworks can be seen in the background.** *Brian Standish*

Left: **Judging from this view, the banker locomotive made a much neater job of exiting the goods station. Are the railway staff on the footplate just posing, or do they think they can get her going again?** *Brian Standish*

The Stourbridge Railway & the Stourbridge Extension

Stourbridge was served by the OWW from 3 May 1852, but much of the Black Country between there and Birmingham had no other railhead. This ignored heavy consumers of raw materials and energetic producers of finished items, who required vast quantities of iron and other materials. News of the Stourbridge Town branch opening spurred local ironmasters to promote the Stourbridge Railway, from a junction with the OWW at Stourbridge (3 miles 35 chains) to Old Hill, via Lye and Cradley Heath. This was to have two branches — one to serve collieries at Hayes Lane and Cradley, the other the New British Iron Co's ironworks at Corngreaves. A second line was also promoted, to extend the Stourbridge Railway 4 miles 65 chains from Old Hill

to a junction with the Stour Valley line near Galton Bridge, with a branch from Cradley Heath to a goods depot at Old Hill. Both lines were authorised, and construction began first on the Stourbridge Railway, which opened to Cradley, with an intermediate station at Lye, on 1 April 1863. The Corngreaves branch came into use on the same day, followed in June by the ¾-mile Hayes Lane branch. Progress to Cradley had been quite rapid, but the next 2¼ miles between Old Hill and Rowley was hard-won. Past Cradley the line is carried on a steep embankment (1 in 51), which required a lot of earth to construct. More than once during construction the embankment collapsed, setting back the opening of the line to Old Hill, which did not take place until 1 January 1866.

The complete railway, to its junction with the Stour Valley line at Galton,

opened on 1 April 1867, with intermediate stations at Rowley, Oldbury & Langley Green, Rood End, and Smethwick Junction. The GWR absorbed the Stourbridge Railway on 1 February 1870. The link between Galton Junction on the Stour Valley line and Smethwick West on the Stourbridge Extension remained in use until January 1961, when it was removed. There was little foresight, however, as, from 6 March 1967, Stourbridge services were diverted into Birmingham New Street, requiring the reinstatement of this link. The situation was partly reversed on 24 September 1995 with the reopening of the line between Smethwick West, which closed, and Birmingham Snow Hill; branded 'the Jewellery line', this had new intermediate stations at Galton Bridge, The Hawthorns and Jewellery Quarter.

Upper left: **A journey along the Stourbridge Railway and Stourbridge Extension Railway. On 5 June 1957 2-6-2T No 5109 works a local towards Stourbridge Junction, with St Mark's Stambermill on the skyline. This portion of the Stourbridge Railway opened to Cradley on 1 April 1863.** *E. J. Dew*

Lower left: **The Stourbridge Railway had one intermediate station, at Lye. This postcard view shows the original buildings. The line to the right led to the goods yard, whilst that to the left was a brickworks' siding.** *Brian Standish*

Right: **More 'temporary' buildings had replaced Lye station by November 1975, but the goods station, enlarged in 1920, was still in use. In 2003 the yard is the base of a company selling packing cases and old railway sleepers.**
Neil Pitts/Author's collection

Below: **The roofline on the extreme right of this February 1967 photograph belongs to a Midland Red bus garage (now a bicycle factory shop), which fixes the location of Cradley Heath goods station (now the station car park). Preserved GWR railcar No W22W stands in the goods yard with a shunter's truck and assorted lorries alongside the goods shed.** *Ron Moss*

Left: **Cradley station was the original terminus of the Stourbridge Railway and from 1 July 1899 was renamed Cradley Heath & Cradley. The platforms were originally staggered, either side of a level crossing, but when the station was modernised in 1983 a new platform was built alongside the original westernmost one. In this view, recorded on 1 June 1983, the goods station seen in the previous photograph has given way to a bus station and car park.** *Chris Morrison*

Left: **The new Cradley Heath station, viewed from the old station's footbridge in March 1984. One of the (raised) level-crossing barriers can be seen on the left.** *Neil Pitts/Author's collection*

Centre left: **The summer of 1983 saw main-line trains diverted along the Stourbridge Railway on Sundays. Here a York–Plymouth HST passes the older portion of Cradley Heath station, then in the process of being demolished.** *Peter J. Green*

Below: **The same buildings are seen intact in this late 1950s view from the other staggered platform across the level crossing. A pannier-tank locomotive is running bunker-first up the gradient, possibly to work on the Halesowen branch.** *Ron Moss*

Right: **The previous photographer's vantage point can be seen across the level crossing at left in this view of Cradley Heath station in the rain in June 1966. At least the canopy didn't leak!** *Andrew Muckley*

Centre right: **An expectant guard looks back as a heavily loaded platform trolley is manœuvred along the platform at Cradley Heath in June 1966. A porter also ponders whether he should offer assistance.**
Andrew Muckley

Bottom right: **Opened on the same day as the Stourbridge Railway was a branch to the New British Iron Co's extensive iron-and steelworks at Corngreaves. This massive site included narrow-gauge (3ft 2½in) lines, some of which were cable-hauled, like that in the foreground in this 1870s view. For many years the New British Iron Co led a perilous financial existence: receivers were appointed in 1887, and the site was split up and sold 10 years later, but the Corngreaves branch would survive until 12 April 1965.**
Author's collection

Left: **The extension of the Stourbridge Railway beyond Cradley Heath was planned from the start but hampered by the construction of two major engineering features. One was a steep embankment to Old Hill with a ruling gradient of 1 in 51. On more than one occasion during its construction the embankment collapsed, setting back the opening of the line to Old Hill until 1 January 1866. Old Hill station is seen acentury later, in June 1966, in a view looking towards Birmingham.** *Andrew Muckley*

Below: **Part of the material used in constructing the embankment between Cradley Heath and Old Hill came from that excavated for Old Hill Tunnel. From atop the western portal in the early 1960s a DMU is seen climbing up from Old Hill station, which is behind and below the houses to the right.** *Ron Moss*

Above: **Braced against subsidence, the same portal of Old Hill Tunnel is seen on 27 April 1963 as '8F' No 48417 leads rebuilt 'West Country' No 34039** *Boscastle* **with a Southampton–Birmingham football special.**
Michael Mensing

Right: **The Stourbridge Extension Railway opened throughout to Galton Junction with the Stour Valley line on 1 April 1867. A Hereford–New Street 'Express Link' service is seen passing Langley Maltings at Langley Green on 3 October 1986.**
Peter Tandy

Left: **There were extensive sidings at Langley Green to serve the major chemical works of Albright & Wilson, founded in 1851. Arthur Albright was the inventor of the safety match, and his works processed phosphorus — key element in these. This is the yard at Langley Green, pictured in November 1977. Behind the photographer was a branch to Oldbury, which opened on 7 November 1884.**
Neil Pitts/Author's collection

Above: **The last station on the Stourbridge Extension Railway was Smethwick Junction. The lines to the right led to the Stour Valley line, whilst those to the left climbed steeply to join the BW&D line. Post-Nationalisation, Smethwick Junction was renamed Smethwick West, seen here in November 1977.**
Neil Pitts/Author's collection

Bottom left: **Ex-GWR No 4988** *Bulwell Hall* **pauses at a well-kept Smethwick West station with a Birmingham–Cardiff train in May 1957. Smethwick West closed upon the opening of the Jewellery line, on 25 September 1995.** *IAL*

6. OLD HILL

On 1 January 1866 the Stourbridge Extension Railway opened to Old Hill. This was an unlikely place for a railway junction, but it once had two lines branching from it that carried services to Birmingham. The idea of a line to Dudley had been promoted as early as 1853 and was revived in 1872 when the Stourbridge Railway obtained powers to build lines between Old Hill, Dudley, and Halesowen, plus a branch to a canal basin at Withymoor (Netherton). Construction was delayed and finally began in the mid-1870s. Both railways opened on 1 March 1878, working from a new station at Old Hill built a little nearer to Stourbridge, in between the junctions of the new lines. Withymoor Basin and branch opened on 10 March 1879.

The junctions at Old Hill did not facilitate through running between the branches, so passage from one line to the other was possible but complicated. From the Dudley line, a train had to pass through Old Hill station on the up line, cross to the down line and then take the Halesowen branch; without an additional locomotive waiting on the down line to be attached to the train, it would then have to back down the branch. Trains from the Halesowen branch had to go through the same procedure in reverse to gain the Dudley line. Little surprise, therefore, that the two lines were operated separately.

Above: **Old Hill was an unlikely place for a railway station, let alone a railway junction. In fact, as at many places, the station wasn't exactly in the town. Old Hill's railway era began with the opening of the Stourbridge Extension Railway to the station of that name on 1 January 1866. Two branches —** **to Dudley and Halesowen — followed on 1 March 1878, on which date a new station, seen here, opened. We won't ask how Ron Moss came to take this shot in 1957. The Stourbridge line curves away to the right, whilst the Halesowen branch goes off to the left.** *Ron Moss*

Centre right: **On the same day in 1957 Ron Moss photographed the main station building at Old Hill. This seems to have been of brick and timber construction, with rather imposing and heavy canopies. The Dudley line can be seen curving away to the right.** *Ron Moss*

Bottom right: **Completing his survey of Old Hill station, Ron Moss took this view of the station approach on 1 September 1963. The extent of the wooden construction is clear. In the background a goods train is being banked up the Stourbridge line, as Midland Red BMMO D7 No 4122 pulls away on a special working.** *Ron Moss*

Right: **The Dudley service had just nine days to run when Ron Moss took this view of one of the line's auto-trains on 6 June 1964. In the distance can be seen the connection to the Halesowen line, as can some of the signalling required to control the locomotive movements associated with operating these two branches.** *Ron Moss*

Below: **The substantial signalbox whose roof was seen in the last photograph is seen to much better advantage in this shot looking down the Stourbridge line along Old Hill Bank, taken on 12 June 1966. In the background a block of system-build flats is inching skywards. The passenger shelter on the signalbox platform, seen in the earlier photographs, has been removed.** *Andrew Muckley*

Above: **The photographer's reason for waiting on Old Hill station on 12 June 1966 was to capture No 7029** *Clun Castle* **storming up Old Hill Bank with an LCGB special from Stourbridge to Banbury. The ruling gradient is 1 in 51.** *Andrew Muckley*

Left: **Approaching Old Hill station,** *Clun Castle* **crosses the by now seldom-used points of the Dudley line and continues up the gradient towards Old Hill Tunnel and on to Banbury on 12 June 1966.** *Andrew Muckley*

The Halesowen line

The Halesowen line left the Stourbridge Railway east of the new station, curving away sharply southeast and terminating at the line's only station, at Halesowen, situated on Mucklow Hill. A separate company — The Halesowen Railway — extended this line 7 miles to a junction with the Midland Railway at Longbridge. This opened on 10 September 1883, with intermediate stations at Hunnington and Rubery. Passenger and goods services were provided jointly by the Midland and GWR. The line's outstanding engineering feature was the 660ft-long Dowery Dell Viaduct, which bore a 10mph speed restriction.

A much delayed branch off the line just north of the station to Halesowen Canal Basin came into use on 2 April 1902; otherwise there were no major changes until the introduction of steam railmotors in March 1905. On 1 July 1905 a new halt was opened at Coombes Holloway, between Old Hill and Halesowen.

Nominally independent, the Halesowen Railway went into receivership in 1904 and was jointly purchased by the GWR and Midland on 26 October 1905. Less than three weeks later, on 10 November 1905, Herbert Austin moved into a redundant tin-printing works at Longbridge, there to develop his car factory, traffic to and from which came to sustain the Halesowen Railway. Austin's workforce expanded tenfold in the first 10 years, the Midland's local services being the main beneficiary. During the Great War Longbridge took on munitions and aircraft work. In February 1915 the Midland opened a new station on the Halesowen branch at Longbridge, close to its junction with the main line, and that summer introduced workmen's services between there and Birmingham New Street.

Service cutbacks caused by the Great War threatened the future of both of Old Hill's branches, but they escaped closure, losing only their Sunday services, from 3 March 1915; these were not restored on the Halesowen line after the war. After the Great War a full weekday service returned to the line, but it began to feel the effects of local bus competition. On 5 December 1927 the GWR withdrew its public passenger service between Old Hill and Halesowen in favour of a replacement bus service provided by the 'Midland Red', in which it was a major shareholder. Coombes Holloway Halt was closed, but Halesowen station remained open to goods and for workmen's services. For a short time, railmotors continued to work to and from Old Hill to connect with the Longbridge workmen's services, but on 31 March 1928 these were also withdrawn, leaving goods services only on the branch.

Midland passenger services between Halesowen and Northfield were withdrawn in April 1919 on the expiry of Longbridge's war contracts, Hunnington and Rubery stations being closed to passengers. Only the workmen's services remained; these continued for almost 40 years and prior to World War 2 were operated by increasingly antiquated stock — four-wheel coaches, clerestory stock etc. The service dwindled to two trains in each direction on weekdays only and was withdrawn from 1 September 1958. The remaining workmen's service, from New Street, was withdrawn on 1 January 1960. From 1 September 1958 the former Halesowen Railway was sustained by freight traffic such as steel pressings for Longbridge and consignments to and from the Blue Bird toffee factory at Hunnington; once the former ceased c1961, line closure was inevitable.

Old Hill–Longbridge proved an attractive route for railtours in the 1960s, and commercial use for parcels and goods continued to Halesowen. A further attraction was that goods trips to Halesowen Canal Basin became one of the last workings for ex-GWR pannier-tank locomotives. The basin's most regular traffic was steel tube from Coombes Wood Steelworks, which was situated along the line. This ceased from 5 June 1967, and Halesowen Goods closed on 9 September 1968. Steel-ingot traffic to Walter Somers Ltd kept part of the line open until 1 October 1969, after which the track was lifted.

Upper right: **Along the Old Hill–Halesowen–Longbridge line. In the 1960s this proved an attractive route for railtours. Here one organised by the Birmingham University Transport Society enters the line on 2 March 1968. Behind the DMU can be seen the cranes and timber in Palmer's Timber Yard.** *Ron Moss*

Bottom right: **A party of schoolboys inspect the Halesowen platform at Old Hill on 30 May 1959. The wooden platform extension was added for the workmen's trains to Longbridge. Palmer's Timber Yard can also be seen to better advantage, as ex-GWR '57xx' 0-6-0PT No 8797 enters the Halesowen branch.** *Ron Moss*

Right: **Steam specials along the Halesowen line were usually banked. On 2 November 1963 Ivatt Class 2MT 2-6-0s Nos 46522 and 46429 bring an SLS special away from Old Hill on its return to Longbridge.** *Ron Moss*

Below: **Tube, parcels and steel traffic kept the Old Hill–Halesowen section of the line in use into the late 1960s. It was also a haven for old pannier tanks; when photographed on 21 June 1966 ex-GWR '57xx' 0-6-0PT No 8718, seen approaching Old Hill with a Halesowen freight, was the oldest ex-GWR standard-gauge locomotive at work on British Railways.**
Andrew Muckley

Above: **A second view of No 8718 on 21 June 1966. The noise seems to have attracted the attention of a young lady clutching a crash helmet — bet there's a scooter not too far away!** *Andrew Muckley*

Left: **A good close-up of 0-6-0PT No 8718 banking a Halesowen train up to Old Hill, again on 21 June 1966. By this date the locomotive's cast numberplate had been removed, her number being stencilled on.**
Andrew Muckley

Above: **Between Old Hill and Halesowen the line passed through Haden Hill Tunnel, which was rarely if ever photographed. In the years before the Great War a train approaches the Halesowen end of the tunnel. In 2003 much of the rolling hillside in the distance has been developed for housing.** *Sandwell Libraries*

Centre right: **Just beyond Halesowen station the line singled and passed under Mucklow Hill. This 1959 photograph was taken from the road bridge above at this point. The goods station can be seen through the smoke in the centre distance.** *Dudley Libraries*

Bottom right: **The Birmingham University Transport Society trip to Halesowen on 2 March 1968. This view shows both the vantage point of the previous photograph and the way in which the trackbed narrowed and was slewed beneath Mucklow Hill.** *Andrew Muckley*

Left: **Evidently a thorough inspection was made of Halesowen station and signalbox on 2 March 1968! In the background is the massive works of Walter Somers Ltd, which remains in 2003 and provides a reference point for anyone trying to find the location of the station. Back in 1968 there is urgency among some of the visitors — perhaps the train is ready to leave.** *Andrew Muckley*

Centre left: **Steel tube, from Coombes Wood Steelworks, made the short journey to Halesowen Canal Basin by water and was then transferred to rail. This was the Basin's most regular traffic, but it ceased from 5 June 1967. Halesowen goods station, whose main building can be seen in the centre background here, closed on 9 September 1968. Steel-ingot traffic to Walter Somers Ltd kept part of the line open until 1 October 1969, after which the track was lifted. It is seen here in its final months.** *Author's collection*

Below: **The outstanding feature of the Halesowen Railway was Dowery Dell Viaduct, which stood midway between the line's two stations at Hunnington and Rubery. Here ex-GWR '74xx' 0-6-0PT No 7435 observes the 10mph speed restriction over the viaduct as she inches her workmen's train off the structure.** *P. J. Shoesmith*

Above left: **These detailed shots by Ron Moss show the slender elegance of Dowery Dell Viaduct's construction. It spanned 660ft and carried its single line 100ft above the valley from which it took its name. Substantially completed by Easter 1881, the viaduct was weight-tested by two 75-ton locomotives on 11 May that year. This view was recorded on 16 April 1961.** *Ron Moss*

Above right: **Dowery Dell Viaduct was supported on eight trestles and stone abutments at each end, one of which is seen in the foreground, right. Regular use of the viaduct began with the opening of the line on 10 September 1883 and ended with the withdrawal of the Longbridge workmen's services on 1 January 1960. Seen here on 17 March 1962, Dowery Dell Viaduct was last used on 4 January 1964 and was dismantled in April 1965.** *Ron Moss*

Above: **Ex-LMS Class 2 MT 2-6-0 No 46522 heads an SLS 'Farewell to the Halesowen Branch' special at Rubery on 2 November 1963. The special has paused on its outward leg for its passengers to have a thorough last look at the station, which had seen its last regular passengers almost 45 years before. Much reduced as a wartime economy from 1 January 1917, by May 1919 services were 'liable to alteration' and 'published by special bills'.** *Ron Moss*

Right: **The return leg of the SLS 'Farewell to the Halesowen Branch' special on 2 November 1963 was headed by Class 2MT 2-6-0 No 46421, seen here at Longbridge station. West Works, built for munitions work during the Great War but later where the classic Mini was made, towers over the scene to the right.** *RonMoss*

Left: **Another view of No 46421 at Longbridge station on 2 November 1963, having just come off the SLS 'Farewell to the Halesowen Branch' special. The bridge ahead carried the Bristol Road over the railway; the buildings above are the North Works, which included the oldest parts of the Longbridge, dating back to its origins as a tin printing works in the 1890s.** *Ron Mos*

Below: **By 1967 what traffic there was to Halesowen Basin and Goods station did not warrant two lines or a platform edge at Old Hill, so the layout was simplified. Ron Moss recorded this operation at an advanced stage on 27 August 1967. Compare this view with Ron's earlier photograph of 30 May 1959 on page 69.** *Ron Moss*

Right: **The line between Old Hill and Halesowen was closed officially on 1 October 1969, and the remaining track and signalling were removed. This view along the cleared trackbed was taken on 2 May 1970, when only the last few signals needed to be collected.** *Ron Moss*

The Dudley line

The double-track Dudley line left the Stourbridge Railway west of the new Old Hill station, veering off sharply northwest. It had an intermediate station at Windmill End and a new one at Netherton, built at its junction with the ex-OWW line. This was named Dudley (South Side) & Netherton, the original OWW Netherton station, ¼ mile south, closing. Following the introduction of steam railmotors on the line in March 1905 three halts were erected, at Old Hill (High Street), Darby End and Baptist End, all coming into use on 21 August 1905. Service cutbacks caused by the Great War threatened the future of the Old Hill–Dudley line. As on the Halesowen line, Sunday services were

withdrawn from 3 March 1915 but were restored after the war ended. Auto-trains replaced the railmotors in the early 1930s and were themselves partially replaced by GWR diesel railcars from October 1940 onwards.

After World War 2 there were some service reductions, but 21 weekday return trips remained, including one through service between Dudley and Birmingham Snow Hill. Throughout the 1950s, however, there was a steady reduction in service, and with the introduction of the winter timetable on 15 September 1952 Windmill End, the only full station on the line, was reduced to the status of unstaffed halt. More cutbacks in 1955 reduced the service still further and saw the end of through services to Birmingham. Hopes

of a brighter future were raised towards the end of 1957 by the replacement of the ageing halt pagodas by modern pre-cast concrete platforms and bus shelters, but yet more service reductions — and the closure from 30 July 1962 of Blower's Green station, with the withdrawal of the Stourbridge-Wolverhampton passenger service — indicated that the line's days were numbered, and passenger services were withdrawn on 15 June 1964. The Dudley line continued in use as a diversionary route and for goods, but Withymoor Basin (Netherton Goods) closed on 5 July 1965, and the route was officially closed on 1 January 1968, although a few trains were recorded using it for a further three months. Lifting of the track was completed by 6 July 1969.

Right: **Along the Old Hill–Dudley line. Train movements at Old Hill were complicated by the lack of a platform for the Dudley service. Services terminated and began from the platforms on the Stourbridge line, requiring the locomotive (if not auto-fitted) to run round its auto-trailer and, at busy times, to reverse its train on to the branch and out of the way. On 3 February 1962 ex-GWR '57xx' 0-6-0PT No 4619 and regular coach W225W are seen at Old Hill; now all they have to do is to get over to the other platform!** *Ron Moss*

Bottom right: **No 4619 runs round its coach at Old Hill on 3 February 1962. Sometimes, when this procedure was finished and the train had moved over to the platform in the foreground, it had to move down the Dudley line for a Stourbridge-bound train to pass. In such instances a special backing signal was provided to allow the Dudley train to reverse wrong-line across the Stourbridge tracks.** *Ron Moss*

Above: **The track arrangements at Old Hill are made clear in this view of the junction with the Dudley line, the special backing signal referred to above being seen centre left. Locomotives on the Dudley trains used the crossover along the Stourbridge line (left) as part of their run-round procedure. On 6 June 1964 — just a week before the last train ran — ex-GWR '64xx' 0-6-0PT No 6434 approaches Old Hill.** *Ron Moss*

Left: **It was not unusual for the locomotives on goods trains from Netherton to reverse to Old Hill. On 30 May 1959 ex-GWR '57xx' 0-6-0PT No 3729 brings a goods train into Old Hill. The Stourbridge line can be seen to the left, while the building just visible on the right can be seen more clearly in the previous photograph.** *Ron Moss*

Above left: **The first stop along the Dudley line from Old Hill was Old Hill (High Street) Halt, which came into use on 21 August 1905. It was reached via Garratt's Lane, the bridge beyond the platforms here spanning that road. This view, looking towards Dudley, was taken in February 1966, 20 months after the last passenger train called.** *Andrew Muckley*

Above right: **Looking back towards Old Hill on 4 August 1962. Ex-GWR '64xx' 0-6-0PT No 6418, being driven from auto-trailer W225W, leaves Old Hill (High Street) Halt down the slight dip in the line before tackling the 1-in-56 gradient up to Old Hill station.** *Ron Moss*

Right: **One year later, on 24 August 1963, a very spruce-looking auto-trailer W221W *Wren* and ex-GWR '64xx' 0-6-0PT No 6424 call at Old Hill (High Street) Halt. Look out — our photographer has been spotted!** *Ron Moss*

Bottom right: **Old Hill (High Street) Halt was actually more convenient for the town than was Old Hill station itself and was thus a popular stop. Also on 24 August 1963, Ron Moss photographed this Dudley-bound service departing.** *Ron Moss*

Above: **Cox's Lane runs parallel and close to Garratt's Lane, but such is the nature of the topography around Old Hill that the Dudley line crossed the former on the level. On 1 November 1958 ex-GWR '64xx' 0-6-0PT No 6418, driven from auto-trailer W160W, has just crossed Cox's Lane Crossing on its way to Dudley.** *Ron Moss*

Centre left: **The next stop on the line to Dudley was Darby End Halt. In history and appearance this was similar to Old Hill (High Street) Halt and was reached via a long flight of steps from Withymoor Road. It is seen 20 months after closure in this February 1966 view looking towards Dudley.** *Andrew Muckley*

Bottom left: **Netherton goods station was reached via a mile-long branch line, which left the Old Hill–Dudley line close to Baptist End Halt. This then ran back in the Old Hill direction, southwards from the Dudley line, until it approached Halesowen Road and the Dudley No 2 Canal. This was the canal/rail trans-shipment shed at Netherton Goods, which closed on 5 July 1965, the route closing officially on 1 January 1968. The trans-shipment shed was demolished in 1967.** *Neil Pitts/Author's collection*

Right: **Past Windmill End, the only intermediate station provided on the Old Hill–Dudley line when it opened on 1 March 1878, the line passed under St Peter's Road, Netherton, from which road bridge Ron Moss photographed an ex-GWR '51xx' 2-6-2T working the line with auto-trailer W160W. Not auto-fitted, the locomotive is leading the coach.** *Ron Moss*

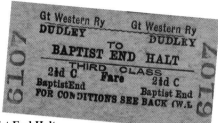

Above: **Baptist End Halt was opened on 21 August 1905. Our journey to Dudley could have been completed on 2 October 1943 using this ticket, which was issued that day.** *Author's collection*

Below: **As seen in the chapter covering Dudley, Old Hill trains used a No 3 bay platform, next to Dudley South signalbox. There, on 28 December 1963, ex-GWR '64xx' 0-6-0PT No 6424 and auto-trailer W254W emit steam from a steam-heating valve as they wait to return to Old Hill.** *Ron Moss*

Right: **Ron Moss must have been leaning against the 'Passengers Must Not Cross the Line …' notice to record this view of the same train on 28 December 1963 in No 3 Bay at Dudley station, which conveys no hint of what was about to be lost.** *Ron Moss*

Centre right: **The line between Old Hill and Dudley was closed officially on 1 January 1968, although a few trains were recorded using it for a further three months. Lifting of the track took place progressively thereafter. Priority was given to removing the junction at Old Hill, which seems to have been completed on 4 August 1968, when this view was recorded. Removal of the entire line was completed by 6 July 1969.** *Ron Moss*

Below left: **The track might have gone, but some of the halts along the line remained. These were the remains of the approach to Old Hill (High Street) Halt before they were removed in the mid-1980s.** *Author*

Below right: **The steps seen above were still negotiable, with caution, which is how this view, looking back along the trackbed towards Old Hill, came to be recorded. Housing now occupies this site.** *Author*

Cover captions:
Front: **On 20 September 1958 No 6001** *King Edward VII* **has almost hauled its rake of nine coaches, forming the 11.45 Birkenhead-Paddington, beneath Trinity Road Bridge, immediately southeast of West Bromwich station. The tower of Trinity Church dominates the skyline behind the backs of houses in Mary Road and Springfield Crescent.** *Michael Mensing*

Rear top: **Early autumn sun casts long shadows as '8F' 2-8-0 No 48415, a Tyseley engine, brings a down freight off the BWD line through Priestfield station at 16.51 on 26 September 1959.** *Michael Mensing*

Rear middle: **A white Morris Minor van twists its way along Powke Lane as '6400' class 0-6-0PT No 6434 pushes an auto-trailer away from Darby End Halt on 14 May 1964. The chalked inscription on the firebox door is the only indication that the closure of the line is a month away.** *Michael Mensing*

Rear bottom: **Whit Sunday 17 May 1964 was a busy day for excursions from the Black Country. Some of those going north went via the GJ line, but at 11.00 'Black 5' 4-6-0 No 44810 had passed through Wolverhampton (High Level) station with its down excursion when it was photographed near Bushbury Lane.** *Michael Mensing*